What Is the Bible

and How Do We

Understand It?

THE JESUS WAY

—SMALL BOOKS *of* RADICAL FAITH—

What Is the Bible

and How Do We Understand It?

DENNIS R. EDWARDS

HERALD
PRESS

Harrisonburg, Virginia

Herald Press
PO Box 866, Harrisonburg, Virginia 22803
www.HeraldPress.com

Library of Congress Cataloging-in-Publication Data
Names: Edwards, Dennis R. (Biblical scholar), author.
Title: What is the Bible and how do we understand it? / Dennis R Edwards.
Description: Harrisonburg : Herald Press, 2019. | Series: The Jesus way:
   small books of radical faith | Includes bibliographical references. |
   Contents: What is the Purpose of the Bible? -- How was the Bible Born?
   -- What is the Center of the Bible? -- What is the Spirit of the Bible?
   -- Who Gets to Interpret the Bible? -- What Impact Does the Bible Make?
   | Summary: "The author offers a succinct and profound investigation of
   Scripture holding up Jesus as the interpretive key and shines light on
   contemporary debates about the Bible. Accessible Jesus-centered theology
   from an Anabaptist perspective"-- Provided by publisher.
Identifiers: LCCN 2019023916 | ISBN 9781513805641 (paperback) | ISBN
   9781513806143 (ebook)
Subjects: LCSH: Bible--Introductions.
Classification: LCC BS475.3 .E335 2019 | DDC 220.6/1--dc23
LC record available at https://lccn.loc.gov/2019023916

WHAT IS THE BIBLE AND HOW DO WE UNDERSTAND IT?
© 2019 by Herald Press, Harrisonburg, Virginia 22803. 800-245-7894.
   All rights reserved.
Library of Congress Control Number: 2019023916
International Standard Book Number: 978-1-5138-0564-1 (paperback);
   978-1-5138-0614-3 (ebook)
Printed in United States of America
Cover and interior design by Reuben Graham

23 22 21 20 19   10 9 8 7 6 5 4 3 2 1

Contents

Introduction to The Jesus Way Series from Herald Press

The Jesus Way is good news for all people, of all times, in all places. Jesus Christ "is before all things, and in him all things hold together"; "in him all the fullness of God was pleased to dwell" (Colossians 1:17, 19). The Jesus Way happens when God's will is done on earth as it is in heaven.

But what does it mean to walk the Jesus Way? How can we who claim the name of Christ reflect the image of God in the twenty-first century? What does it mean to live out and proclaim the good news of reconciliation in Christ?

The Jesus Way: Small Books of Radical Faith offers concise, practical theology that helps readers encounter big questions about God's work in the world. Grounded in a Christ-centered reading of Scripture and a commitment to reconciliation, the series aims to enliven the service and embolden the witness of people who follow Jesus. The volumes in the series are written by a diverse community of internationally renowned pastors, scholars, and practitioners committed to the way of Jesus.

The Jesus Way series is rooted in Anabaptism, a Christian tradition that prioritizes following Jesus, loving enemies, and creating faithful communities. During the Protestant Reformation of the 1500s, early Anabaptists who began meeting for worship emphasized discipleship in addition to belief, baptized adults instead of infants, and pledged their allegiance to God over loyalty to the state. Early Anabaptists were martyred for their radical faith, and they went to their deaths without violently resisting their accusers.

Today more than two million Anabaptist Christians worship in more than one hundred countries around the globe. They include Mennonites, Amish, Brethren in Christ, and Hutterites. Many other Christians committed to Anabaptist beliefs and practices remain in church communities in other traditions.

Following Jesus means turning from sin, renouncing violence, seeking justice, believing in the reconciling power of God, and living in the power of the Holy Spirit. The Jesus Way liberates us from conformity to the world and heals broken places. It shines light on evil and restores all things.

Join Christ-followers around the world as we seek the Jesus Way.

Introduction

The Bible has given exuberant joy, certain comfort, inspiration, guidance, and courage to countless numbers of people. Over the course of centuries, bodies have been healed, bad habits broken, families reconciled, communities positively transformed, and unjust laws overturned because of fiery faith in God that was stoked by the Bible. Space and time do not allow for discussion of all the good things the Bible has inspired: great works of art; humanitarian efforts to eliminate sickness, poverty, and injustice; the creation of hospitals, churches, schools, and other institutions for human flourishing. Virtually limitless good work has flowed from a broad cross-section of people reading the Bible and acting upon its teachings.

The Bible has also provoked wars. More accurately, people have fought wars because of their understanding of the Bible's teachings. Some husbands have verbally and physically abused their wives with apparent justification from the Bible. Some parents have traumatized their children through beatings and rigid authoritarianism based on Bible verses. White Christians in the New World found justification for purchasing and owning Black people in passages of the Bible. Origen of Alexandria (AD 184–253), a church father, was rumored to have castrated himself based on his understanding of verses in the Bible and his longing to be liberated from sexual temptation. While the story may be mythical, a fringe movement of Christians in the Middle Ages, known as flagellants, did whip their own bodies in order to punish themselves for sin. Violence—against others and against the self—has resulted from some people's understanding of the Bible. The Bible has been a source of pain for many.

How can the Bible provoke such strong and opposite reactions? How can Scripture so powerfully inspire the best in humans—and be used to justify the worst? Given the ways that the Bible has been used as well as misused, we must understand, as best we can, what the Bible is. Some people may find studying the Bible intimidating, especially if they reckon that it requires a monumental degree of faith or an extraordinary level of formal education. Yet without study, the Bible could end up an icon, idol, or curio, gathering dust on a shelf or coffee table. "The Bible is much more easily reverenced than read," writes theologian Peter J. Gomes.[1]

My appreciation for Scripture has grown over the years. As a child I attended a storefront church that expected attendees to know the Scriptures, even to the point of memorizing much of it. Although I memorized Bible passages, I was not taught how to understand the Scriptures for myself. Interpretation of the Bible was something that the preacher did; the listeners were required to obey. The Bible was full of mysteries, and I did not have the tools to unravel them.

Thus I began a lifelong quest to learn God's Word so that I could obey it and teach it to others. Even more than for employment opportunities, doctoral studies became part of my personal quest for understanding. Today as I study the Scriptures, I find that there is always more to discover about God, about the world from which the Bible emerged, about the contemporary world, and about myself, as I desire to be a faithful follower of Jesus Christ.

Christians view the Bible as Holy Scripture, the Word of God, and we use those terms interchangeably. We believe the Bible to be inspired by God and authoritative for our faith and life. Even so, it was written and compiled by human beings. And despite the Bible's ubiquity in North America, many people know little about its purpose and origin.

The Bible is a love story that moves from the creation of the universe (Genesis) to a new creation (Revelation). In chapter 1 of this book, we look at the Bible as an overarching story—a story that must be kept in mind when reading individual parts of the Bible, even the confusing and distressing parts. Scripture is often more descriptive than prescriptive, and the various mini-stories within the larger biblical story teach us about God and about ourselves. When we consider the grand story of the Bible, it is fair to say that the Bible's purpose is revelatory—to introduce us to God—and also to help us understand how to relate to God and to each other.

In chapter 2, I outline the formation and canonization of the Bible, noting the Bible's genres while also mentioning the contents of major sections of the Bible. (Throughout the book, key terms appear in bold and are defined in the glossary.) I then discuss some of the challenges of making contemporary translations of the Bible.

Chapter 3 asserts that Jesus Christ is the focal point of all of Scripture. Even the words written long before he showed up on earth point to him in some way. The life of Jesus, as described in the Gospels, gives us a picture of the character of God and also instructs us how to live a life of love for God and others.

Chapter 4 explains that since the Holy Spirit is understood to have been active in the writing of the Bible, we can trust that the Spirit is also active in our understanding of the Bible. Anyone can analyze the Bible, because it contains writings that can be studied like all other writings—ancient or modern. But when readers recognize and honor the Holy Spirit, they can discover insights about God, humanity, and even themselves. Through the Holy Spirit, followers of Jesus can navigate contemporary issues that the Bible does not directly address. The Bible, under the guidance of the Holy Spirit, gives spiritual wisdom that is applicable in modern times.

Chapter 5 urges that study of the Bible be done within a community. While personal study of the Bible is helpful and good, studying it in conversation with other students of the Scriptures is even better. Those students certainly include one's peers, but should also include readers from the past, as there is much written work that has informed Christians for centuries. Other conversation partners include Christians from historically marginalized groups, whose perspectives often coincide with those of the first readers of the Bible. Those first readers were themselves seemingly insignificant actors on the human stage.

The Scriptures not only give us information but can also be a catalyst of our transformation, a truth we look at in chapter 6. Communities of Jesus-followers will make a positive impact in the world by embodying the teachings of Scripture. In this chapter we consider practical guidelines for the study of Scripture passages.

Our goal is not only to read the Bible but to understand it as best we can. How might our understanding of the Bible transform us? We turn now to consider the purpose of the Bible, reflecting on the story it tells and considering our place in that story.

1

What Is the Purpose of the Bible?

Sometimes when I preach, I claim that the Bible is not a list of rules but a love story. After one service in which I made such an assertion, a woman approached me, her preadolescent children at her side, to express her disagreement. She believed the Bible is a rule book and that I had diminished its authority by calling it a love story.

I am sympathetic to a mother's need for rules for her children and her desire to see the Bible as the source of those rules. Perhaps she had grown up with the Bible serving such a purpose. I did not try to change her mind, and we parted that day with our differing perspectives, yet still respecting each other's point of view. In another church where I'd made the same assertion—that the Bible is a love story—a woman approached me after the service to say how much that description had warmed her heart and given her comfort.

I insist that the Bible is a love story, but I don't intend for that to sound like sappy sentimentality. The notion of the Bible's love story held appeal for believers who lived centuries ago. For example, an early Anabaptist Christian, Peter Riedeman, wrote in 1542 that it has always been God's desire to be in relationship with creation: "It is his will to be our God and Father, and that we should be his people and loved children, and that he desires through Christ to fill us at all times with every divine blessing and with all that is good."[1] This perspective permeates the Bible, even though not every section or verse we read has love in the foreground.

Because the Bible is an eclectic collection of writings, it can be a bit like the proverbial elephant being examined by people who cannot see. In that story, each person, touching only a part of the elephant, generalizes their findings and winds up making assumptions about the entire elephant. If one focuses on rules in the Bible, the Bible will become a rule book. If one focuses exclusively on verses about happiness and joy, the Bible will become a manual for personal fulfillment on earth. If one focuses on verses about sin and judgment, the Bible will become a source of condemnation of others and possibly of oneself as well.

But the Bible is more than just any one of those parts, and even more than the *sum* of those parts. The various writings that make up the Bible—including the rules, the songs, the promises, the short and long stories, and the admonitions, along with the pronouncements of judgment—conspire to tell a story. The Bible tells a story, even though it consists of parts that aren't narrative and don't have a convenient "beginning, middle, end" flow to them. Ghanaian scholar Kwame Bediako declares that "Scripture is not just a holy book from which we extract teaching and biblical principles. Rather, it is a story in which we participate."[2] The grand story of the Bible is one of love: God's love for humanity and God's efforts to create a safe, secure, and satisfying existence for humans in harmonious relationship with God and each other.

THE BIBLE TELLS A STORY

If you've ever tried to read the Bible from cover to cover, perhaps as a New Year's resolution, you probably found it pretty interesting for the first several days as you went through Genesis and Exodus. But when you got to Leviticus, things might have slowed down dramatically!

Although the Bible tells a story, it is not all stylistically narrative. New Testament scholar Richard Bauckham observes, "While not all Scripture is generically narrative, . . . the story Scripture tells, from creation to new creation, is the unifying element that holds literature of other genres together with narrative in an intelligible whole."[3] Bauckham's description of the biblical story as one of "creation to new creation" resonates with the notion that the Bible is a love story. At the center of that love story is Jesus; more on that idea in chapter 3. Right now, it is helpful to consider what may be the Bible's grand story.

The idea that the Bible has a grand, overarching story might be new to some people, especially if they're accustomed to viewing the Bible as a random collection of tales and truisms. But the Bible does tell a story, and offering an overarching story may prove especially helpful when you are talking to someone who is unfamiliar with the Bible. Most popular Christian summaries of the Bible's story follow this pattern: creation, fall, redemption, and consummation. The world is created (Genesis 1–2); humans fall into sin (Genesis 3); Jesus comes to redeem humanity (explained in Paul's letters); and history is wrapped up when Jesus returns to earth (Revelation).

Certainly, something like that movement is found in the Bible. Yet emphasizing this creation-fall-redemption-consummation pattern tends to magnify a small part of the Bible (Genesis 3) while omitting a large portion of the Old Testament (such as Exodus, Psalms, Proverbs, historical books, and the Prophets). It also downplays the life of Jesus on earth while focusing almost exclusively on the apostle Paul's letters.

In Matthew's gospel, Jesus is called Emmanuel, or "God with us" (Matthew 1:23). In John's gospel, we read that Jesus is the Word of God who made his home among human beings (John 1:14). The Gospels stress the life and teachings of Jesus and show him to be the most significant witness of who God is and what God is about (Hebrews 1:1-4). The summary of Scripture that focuses on creation, fall, redemption, and consummation correctly highlights the death and resurrection of Jesus—but it says next to nothing about his earthly ministry. If Jesus is the center of Scripture, as we will look at in chapter 3, then a different narrative might be more helpful.

There's another way to consider the biblical data, and I invite you to ponder this Jesus-centered version of the grand story of the Bible. This story of the Bible highlights three topics that are introduced in the Old Testament and then reversed in order in the New Testament. In the Old Testament, the story unfolds the themes of creation, salvation, and the kingdom of God. That movement is evident through the drama surrounding the people of Israel. When we get to the New Testament, the story plays out in reverse, but with Jesus as the key. Jesus not only preaches and teaches about the kingdom of God, but is shown to be the source of ultimate salvation. He is also the one who ushers in God's new creation. Love consistently motivates God, who is the central character in the Bible's drama and is presented as Creator, Savior, and King.

The titles Creator, Savior, and King also apply to Jesus. We discover that Jesus is God in flesh, which gives human beings a clearer picture of what God is like. God is the Creator, who establishes and sustains the world (John 1:3; Colossians 1:16). Jesus is Savior, who rescues humanity from sin and death (Colossians 1:13; Romans 5:9-10). Jesus is also King, sovereign over all creation (1 Corinthians 15:24-25; Ephesians 1:22; 1 Timothy 1:16-17; 1 Peter 3:22). Through Jesus, God sent the Holy Spirit to empower all who follow Jesus. The Holy Spirit works within and among the followers of Jesus to help us know God better as history advances toward the new creation.

Let's look at each of these themes in a bit more detail.

FROM CREATION TO SALVATION TO THE KINGDOM

The Bible's story begins with God's creation of the heavens and the earth (Genesis 1:1-2). I recognize that not all Bible readers take the beginning of Genesis to be historical writing, and my point here is not to debate the specifics of the creation account. Rather, it is to suggest that the story introduces readers to a God who has power over everything yet chooses to live in harmony with human beings. Genesis portrays God not only as Creator but also as Savior, who fashioned the world from nothing and did not leave it in a formless and chaotic condition. In Genesis 1, each act of creation begins with the words "and God said." Genesis communicates that God is king over all, creating by his authoritative word. Right from the start of the Bible, God is shown to be Creator, Savior, and King. Creation also displays God's love, evident in how everything that God made was declared to be good (Genesis 1:31) and was for the benefit of humanity, who was made in the likeness of God

(vv. 26-27). As theologian Willie James Jennings observes, "A Christian doctrine of creation is first a doctrine of place and people, of divine love and divine touch, of human presence and embrace, and of divine and human interaction."[4] Humans were to live in harmony with God and each other, under God's care in an ideal environment (Genesis 2:4-25).

Salvation, or deliverance, is a key theme of the second book of the Bible. Exodus is largely the story of God working through Moses to rescue Israel out of slavery in Egypt. As I noted earlier, Christians usually tell the story of the Bible as moving from creation to the fall, which is the disobedience of Adam and Eve in the garden of Eden. It is true that according to Genesis, the prototypical humans not only disobeyed God but tried to usurp God's role by being "like God" (Genesis 3:5). Yet the story of Adam and Eve is not central in the Old Testament. In fact, the Old Testament itself rarely reflects on that story.[5] The serpent of Genesis 3:1 is not explicitly identified as the devil, or Satan, in the Old Testament (Revelation 20:2 makes the connection). Satan's origin is a mystery. Even though some have attempted to identify Satan with the king of Babylon who is castigated in Isaiah 14:3-23, that identification is unlikely.

Genesis does, however, recount how human rebellion against God is evil, pulling the world toward chaos, resulting in murder (Genesis 4:8) and all manner of wickedness (6:5). The point of Genesis is not primarily about the origins of evil but about the manifestations of sin as well as the need to be free of sin.

By contrast, the event frequently recounted in the Old Testament—virtually countless times—is Israel's deliverance from Egypt. Here are a few examples from different parts of the Old Testament:

I am the LORD your God, who brought you out of the land of Egypt, out of the house of slavery. (Exodus 20:2)

For it is the LORD our God who brought us and our ancestors up from the land of Egypt, out of the house of slavery, and who did those great signs in our sight. He protected us along all the way that we went, and among all the peoples through whom we passed. (Joshua 24:17)

And [Samuel] said to them, "Thus says the LORD, the God of Israel, 'I brought up Israel out of Egypt, and I rescued you from the hand of the Egyptians and from the hand of all the kingdoms that were oppressing you.'" (1 Samuel 10:18)

"And now, O Lord our God, who brought your people out of the land of Egypt with a mighty hand and made your name renowned even to this day—we have sinned, we have done wickedly." (Daniel 9:15)

These verses are but a small sample of the many places in which the Old Testament mentions God's deliverance of Israel out of Egypt. The book of Exodus foreshadows the ministry of Jesus in several ways, preparing readers to understand what it means for Jesus to be Savior.

Seeing God as one who saves will also enhance our appreciation of what God is like. It is common for people to have a harsh image of God: an angry old monarch, seated on his throne with folded arms, ready to punish or kill anyone who steps out of line. Yet the notion of God as Savior conjures different images. Rather than seeing the God of the Old Testament as cruel and vindictive, we might be able to view God as motivated by love toward creation, with arms outstretched to receive us, not folded in disappointment.

Seeing the emphasis on salvation throughout Scripture may help us stop pitting the God of the Old Testament against

Jesus. It is commonplace to hear people say that Jesus is loving and kind, while the God of the Old Testament is judgmental and even capricious. But the God who saves in the Old Testament is the same God who saves in the New Testament.

African Americans have long understood God to be Savior, having seen ourselves in the exodus story. While white slave owners typically appealed to the Bible to justify slavery, Black slaves and their descendants believed that the God revealed in the Bible is the Savior who rescues people out of slavery.

Additionally, Exodus prepares us for the important idea that sin involves slavery. Pharaoh, the antagonist in the early part of Exodus, had influence over the structures that bound the Israelites. In that regard, Pharaoh is like Satan. The Bible depicts Satan, the devil, as having influence over the structures that affect human beings (Ephesians 2:2). Human beings are victimized by evil, often evident in the way societies are structured. Slavery, patriarchy, and fascism are examples of oppressive systems that prevent human flourishing. Those systems are sinful, supported through violence and intimidation. Everyone caught up in evil systems—those who perpetuate them, as well as those who are victimized by them—needs to be liberated. Consequently, sin is not only the evil thoughts and deeds that individuals commit; sin is the pervasive power that damages and corrupts God's creation.

For Israel to be free from Egyptian slavery, Pharaoh's influence needed to end. Similarly, for humanity to be free of evil, sin and the devil's influence must be stopped. The New Testament makes this point explicitly: "The Son of God [Jesus] was revealed for this purpose, to destroy the works of the devil" (1 John 3:8), and "Since, therefore, the children share flesh and blood, he himself likewise shared the same things, so that through death he might destroy the one who has the power of death, that is, the devil, and free those who all their lives were held in slavery by the fear of death" (Hebrews 2:14-15). The exodus of the people of Israel out of Egypt is the pivotal event in the Old Testament, intended to display God's sovereignty. Not only does God defeat the Egyptians and their supposed deities; he gives his people, through Moses, the Ten Commandments.

The Ten Commandments are part of God's covenant, or pact, with Israel, and become their basic guide for honoring God as king. With God as their king, Israel would be a light to all other nations (Isaiah 42:6). Sadly, Israel, for the most part, would eventually reject God's kingship. After years of nomadic life in the wilderness, the people of Israel settled into what was called the Promised Land. During that time, they had various leaders who attempted to keep the people focused on God as king, but the people, observing the pattern of other nations, sought a human king for themselves. In 1 Samuel 8:4-9, it is clear that Israel's request for a human king was a rejection of God as the people's king. But God does not give up on humanity. God promises to work through Israel's second king, David: "I will not take my steadfast love from him" (2 Samuel 7:15). God will establish his kingship through a descendant of King David.

Israel's monarchy proved to be disastrous. Most of the kings were responsible for the nation's idolatry. The nation even split into two kingdoms, one in the north and one in the south. The nation nearly disappeared; it was overtaken by the Assyrians (in the north) and the Babylonians (in the south). Prior to and even during foreign invasion, God continually sent prophets to remind the people that God is their king. The prophets pleaded for the people to repent—to turn back to God (see examples in Ezekiel 14:6; Hosea 6:1; Joel 2:13). The

Old Testament ends with the expectation that some descendant of David will arrive to be an instrumental part of God's work of deliverance and restoration. That is why the New Testament opens with a genealogy of Jesus Christ, connecting him to King David (Matthew 1:1-17).

FROM THE KINGDOM TO SALVATION TO THE NEW CREATION

Jesus, then, is the hinge on which the story of the Bible swings. We have come through creation, to salvation, to a kingdom, and now Jesus ushers in the true kingdom, eternal salvation, and the new creation. When Jesus began his three-year public ministry by preaching the good news that the kingdom of God is near, he sounded like the Old Testament prophets who urged people to repent (Matthew 4:17; Mark 1:15). Often using parables, Jesus described what God's kingdom is like (see, for example, Luke 13:18-21) while demonstrating the character and nature of God (John 1:14; 14:8-11). As he taught, Jesus displayed the kingdom's nearness by performing miraculous signs, including healing sick people (as in Matthew 4:23; Luke 4:18-19).

The Gospels stress that Jesus is the promised son of David, called "Christ," which is the Greek translation of the Hebrew word *Messiah*. Messiah means "anointed one," and Jesus is the one anointed to be king over all. The reign of Jesus, however, is markedly different from that of ordinary monarchs, as he does not depend on violence or coercion (Matthew 20:25). In fact, Jesus said that he came "not to be served but to serve" (Mark 10:45).

Jesus also communicated that his mission on earth included suffering, death, and resurrection (Mark 8:31). With his death, Jesus demonstrated the self-emptying character of God

(Philippians 2:6-8). Jesus also provided salvation for all who would follow him as king. The New Testament uses many images and metaphors to describe salvation—far too many to discuss here. One key image, however, is that of ransom (see, for example, Mark 10:45; 1 Peter 1:18; 1 Timothy 2:6). To people familiar with slavery, as those in the first century surely were, ransom meant manumission—liberation from captivity—which is salvation. Through the death and resurrection of Jesus, humans can find forgiveness for the sins they've committed and also be set free from sin's domination. Through the death and resurrection of Jesus, God establishes that Jesus is king (Philippians 2:9-11).

The rest of the New Testament—the book of Acts through Revelation—reflects upon the life, death, and resurrection of Jesus while also guiding the followers of Jesus toward life in God's new creation. Those writings address various questions that early believers had as well as situations that they faced, and also speak to our present contexts. Revelation ends with the downfall of secular empires and the emergence of idyllic images of God's new city. From Genesis to Revelation, the overarching story moves from creation to salvation to the kingdom of God, then from the kingdom to salvation to new creation.

THE BIBLE REVEALS GOD, WHO WANTS OUR FAITHFUL ALLEGIANCE

Psalm 119 is the longest chapter in the Bible. It is a poem that celebrates God's word. It is also an example of tremendous literary creativity. The psalm is a masterful acrostic poem. There are twenty-two sections, each containing eight verses, for a total of 176 verses. There are twenty-two letters in the Hebrew Bible, and each set of eight verses starts with a successive letter of the alphabet. In other words, verses 1-8 all start with *aleph*, the first letter of the Hebrew alphabet. Verses 9-16 each start with *beth*, the second letter, and so on. The creative writer of Psalm 119 reveals some of the character of God, such as God's love: "Let your steadfast love become my comfort according to your promise to your servant" (v. 76). But the psalm is mainly a tribute to God's word, noting the practical benefits of devotion: "Your word is a lamp to my feet and a light to my path" (v. 105). Psalm 119 is an example of how the Bible reveals the God who is not distant but near, who relates lovingly to creation and is eager for creation's faithful allegiance. Faithful allegiance means a wholehearted commitment to knowing and following God.

As I mentioned in the introduction, it is fair to say that the Bible's purpose is revelatory—to introduce us to God—and also to help us understand how to relate to God and to each other. While the Bible isn't a psychology book, it does guide us toward flourishing and wholeness. Human beings are meant to have an invigorating relationship with God through faith in Jesus Christ. We are designed for love: to be loved by God, to love God, and to love others.

Within the grand story of the Bible there are many varied and sometimes confusing passages. Yet even the cryptic passages can, in some way, inform us about God and expose realities about ourselves. In the next few chapters I give some guidance on how we might read, understand, and apply the various parts of the Bible, including the difficult ones.

The Bible is not merely a story conveying information; it presents itself as revelation. One of the writings attributed to the apostle Paul claims that "all scripture is inspired by God and is useful for teaching, for reproof, for correction, and for training in righteousness, so that everyone who belongs to God may be proficient, equipped for every good work"

(2 Timothy 3:16-17). The word *scripture* in this passage mainly refers to the Old Testament, but the point is that God speaks through words written by humans and inspired by the Spirit. And the written Word is designed for the flourishing of the reader.

God communicates to us through the Bible, and the key to receiving and understanding God's communication is Jesus. But before we focus on Jesus as the key, or center, of the Bible, it is helpful to understand some of how the Bible became the book that we now possess.

2

How Was the Bible Born?

We know the Bible as a perennially bestselling, readily available book that a person can grab for free from a hotel nightstand. Bibles come leather-bound, in paperback, and digitally downloaded onto smartphones, on which the styles and sizes of fonts can be adjusted in seconds. Some Bibles come with study notes, tailored to specific situations in life.

But the Bible did not fall out of the sky. It was not produced as a single written work, nor developed within a short span of time. The Bible we know today is the fruit of many people's labor in concert with the Holy Spirit over many years. The Bible, the written Word of God, mirrors the Christian understanding of Jesus Christ, the incarnate Word of God. John refers to Jesus as "the Word" (John 1:1) and the word of Life (1 John 1:1). Christians have long pondered the mystery of Jesus being the Word of God who is fully divine but also fully human (John 1:14). The Bible is the product of humans under the guidance of the Holy Spirit, making it a divine and human entity. We should not be alarmed by the fact that human minds, demonstrating varying degrees of literary skill, along with human hands, from different parts of the ancient world, were used to develop the Bible. Human fingerprints on the written Word of God should not be taken to mean that the voice of God is missing or even muted. God's presence often shows up in human activity. While God certainly acts independently of human beings, God also delights to involve human beings in divine work. The Bible is the supreme example of divine-human collaboration.

The Bible is largely the product of storytelling—people passing along stories and lessons from one generation to the next. At various points in time, stories were written down and collected. Other writings, such as letters, became part of the collection. The Bible's current form portrays the efforts of faithful people to arrange the book in a helpful way. It is possible to remove the veil of mystery that shrouds the Bible without disrespecting it. In fact, learning the rich history of Scripture can increase our love and appreciation of it. Let's look briefly at how the Bible developed.

THE BIBLE IS A LIBRARY

The word *Bible* comes from a Greek word, *biblion*, sometimes translated as "scroll" (see Luke 4:17, 20). An ancient *biblion* was a scroll made of papyrus (*byblos* in Greek). Even though we know the Bible as a single book, it is actually a collection of writings. The Bible can be thought of as a library, because it consists of several books put together over time, and also because different sections of the Bible contain different styles of writing. There is poetry, found in songs, proverbial words of wisdom, and prophetic oracles. There are narratives, which focus on the activities of God as well as the exploits of innumerable men, women, and children. Readers discover plenty of lengthy speeches, long lists of names, and many numerical details. Four presentations of the life of Jesus—the Gospels— are followed by stories of the growing movement of Jesus-followers. After that there are letters directed to specific people and communities, along with some letters whose initial recipients remain a mystery.

The Bible is a collection, but it is not a random one. Its coherence is surely thanks to its primary subject, God, but also thanks to the grand saga of God guiding humanity into a community built on love.

The books of the Bible were assembled deliberately by people who believed in God and viewed the Bible as revelation from God. The two major sections of the Bible are popularly known as the Old Testament and the New Testament. Largely out of respect for Jewish people, the Old Testament is sometimes called the **Hebrew Bible**, even though there are portions written in Aramaic. It should come as no surprise that many Jews refer to the Old Testament simply as "the Bible." There is another common term for the Old Testament used by Jewish people and scholars: **Tanak** (or Tanach). Tanak is an acronym reflecting the three main sections of the Jewish arrangement of the Old Testament: *T* for **Torah** (Hebrew for "instruction"), *N* for Nevi'im (Prophets), and *K* for Ketuvim (Writings). The vowel *a* is supplied between the consonants TNK so that it reads as Tanak.

The Torah consists of the first five books of the Old Testament: Genesis, Exodus, Leviticus, Numbers, and Deuteronomy. Note that those English names are derived from Greek.

In the Hebrew Bible, the books are called according to the first few words of the writing (for example, Genesis is known as *bereshit*, "in the beginning"). The Greek designation of these five books is **Pentateuch**, which means "five scrolls." The Torah is largely the story of how the people of Israel came to be. The Torah opens with creation and the birth of civilization. It gives brief biographies of Israel's matriarchs and patriarchs, like Sarah and Abraham, Rebecca and Isaac, and Leah, Rachel, and Jacob. Exodus primarily describes Israel's deliverance from slavery in Egypt under the leadership of Moses, along with receipt of the Ten Commandments. Leviticus, in large part, describes the rituals that would help create a cohesive community under God. Numbers details various episodes within Israel's journey through the wilderness. Deuteronomy consists largely of speeches by Moses just prior to his death, emphasizing the need for Israel's fidelity to the Torah as the nation prepares to enter the Promised Land. The book also poignantly recounts the death of Moses, with God as the only witness to his burial plot (Deuteronomy 34:5-6).

The second section of the Tanak, Nevi'im (Prophets), consists of the following books: Joshua, Judges, 1 & 2 Samuel, 1 & 2 Kings, Isaiah, Jeremiah, and Ezekiel, along with the Minor Prophets—so named because of the relatively short length of these writings, not because of any lack of importance. The Minor Prophets are Hosea, Joel, Amos, Obadiah, Jonah, Micah, Nahum, Habakkuk, Zephaniah, Haggai, Zechariah, and Malachi. These books start with the history of Israel's transition from wandering in the desert to settling in the Promised Land and developing a monarchy. We are introduced to many important characters, such as Joshua, who succeeded Moses, as well as the notable King David. Under the monarchy, the people of God struggled to live according to the Torah. One persistent temptation was to worship multiple gods, as was the custom of neighboring nations of the ancient Near East. Consequently, prophets became increasingly prominent. At great personal risk, the prophets constantly urged God's people to "return," or "repent," as they strived to revive fidelity to the one true God (see Isaiah 31:6; Jeremiah 3:12; Hosea 14:1).

The third section, Ketuvim, is something of a catch-all category encompassing several different styles of writings. It includes Psalms, Proverbs, Job, Song of Solomon, Ruth, Lamentations, Ecclesiastes, Esther, Daniel, Ezra, Nehemiah, and 1 & 2 Chronicles.

Ancient Hebrew and Aramaic had no vowels, only consonants. Over time, however, various markings, including those signifying vowels, were added to the consonantal text of the Hebrew Bible. Those who read the Tanak today in the original languages typically read from what is known as the **Masoretic Text**. That text was developed in the Middle Ages when Jewish scribes produced the various markings. The Masoretic Text forms the basis of our modern translations of the Old Testament.

There is another important version of the Jewish Scriptures, however, that not only helps in developing modern translations but also served many of the earliest Christian believers. As a result of Israel's exile into Babylon and their eventual release by the Persian king Cyrus, Jewish culture developed both inside and outside of the Promised Land. The Greeks became dominant, and about two hundred years before the birth of Christ, diaspora Jews under Hellenism (the pervasive influence of Greek culture) developed Greek translations of the Hebrew Bible called the **Septuagint**. Many of the New Testament's quotations of the Old Testament come directly from the

Septuagint. We can think of the Septuagint as the Bible that the apostles knew.

The Septuagint varies from the Masoretic Text in several ways. The most noteworthy difference is the presence of fifteen writings (in the form of separate books as well as additions to known books) that are collectively called the **Apocrypha**.[1] Apocrypha means "hidden," but these books are not secret. As part of the Septuagint, they were written in Greek, and were not part of the original Tanak. The Masoretic Text does not contain these writings. Roman Catholics include the apocryphal books in their Bibles with the designation **deuterocanonical**, suggesting a secondary status as compared to the rest of the books of the Bible. The Orthodox Church also includes these books as part of the "longer canon," giving them the same status as the rest of the Old Testament.

The New Testament is a collection of writings that likely date from the AD 40s to possibly the AD 90s.[2] The New Testament was written in the same Greek as the Septuagint and opens with the Gospels (Matthew, Mark, Luke, and John). The Gospels communicate teachings of Jesus with varying degrees of details about his life on earth. The Gospels are not full biographies like those we might be familiar with in our time. The Gospels share history about Jesus, along with particular teachings and stories, in order to emphasize theological ideas unique to each book.

For example, Matthew opens with the Lord's genealogy, presenting Jesus with clear connections to the Old Testament. Matthew's audience was likely mostly Jewish, so the presentation of Jesus especially resonated with them. Mark was likely written to largely non-Jewish (Gentile) Christians who were facing a degree of persecution because of their faith. Mark's focus on a suffering Savior in many ways spoke uniquely to his first readers. Luke wrote to a Greek (Gentile) patron and tells his story in much the way an investigative journalist might, seeking eyewitnesses and striving to include historical details (see Luke 1:1-4). John is younger than the other three gospels, deviates from their storytelling pattern, and emphasizes the divinity of Jesus even more than the others.

After the four Gospels is the book of Acts, written by the same person who wrote the Gospel according to Luke, and addressed to the same recipient, a man named Theophilus (Acts 1:1). The Holy Spirit is the prominent character in the book, carrying on the ministry of Jesus after his resurrection and ascension. The book details how the early followers of Jesus coalesced into a movement under the impetus of the Holy Spirit. The book of Acts also introduces Saul of Tarsus, more popularly known as the apostle Paul, who becomes the most prominent voice in the growing Christian movement. His writings, letters addressed to various people and congregations, make up nearly half of the entire New Testament (Romans, 1 & 2 Corinthians, Galatians, Ephesians, Philippians, Colossians, 1 & 2 Thessalonians, 1 & 2 Timothy, Titus, and Philemon). Paul's letters are arranged in order of length, not chronologically.

After the Pauline letters are the general epistles (Hebrews, James, 1 & 2 Peter, 1, 2, & 3 John, Jude). These letters were written to various audiences, some of whom are unknown to us. Yet we know that some, like the original recipients of 1 Peter, were facing persecution. The general epistles urge faithfulness to Jesus while warning against apostasy.

The final book of the Bible, Revelation, is an example of **apocalyptic writing**, a genre that was most prevalent from about 250 BC to AD 250. Interpretations of the book of Revelation have varied greatly, largely because of confusion over how to understand apocalyptic literature. Revelation, addressed to seven churches, teaches perseverance through trials, warns of corrupt governments, and ends with the hope of God's new creation.

THE CANON

Canon derives from a Greek word, *kanōn*, which means "rule" or "standard." With respect to the Bible, *canon* refers to the books that are viewed as authoritative. We should view canonization as a process rather than an event. Neither Judaism nor Christianity started with a fixed list of writings; rather, each faith developed and refined its set of sacred texts as time went on. Judaism's process of canonization ended sometime around the second century AD, with the inclusion of the books of the Tanak noted above but not the Apocrypha.

Christians have always relied on the Hebrew Scriptures, but within a couple of hundred years of the church's existence, many Christian writings emerged to complement what became known as the Old Testament. However, not all of these new Christian writings reflected the character or consistency of what the church had been teaching and practicing from its earliest days. Some writings reflected ideas that were deemed heretical, such as the denial of the divinity or humanity of Jesus.

During the fourth century, church leaders met to ratify the writings that should be considered authoritative. Their criteria were basically threefold.

1. Apostolicity. Was the book written by an apostle of Jesus? In this case, *apostle* refers not only to one of the twelve original apostles who first followed Jesus during his life on earth, but also to someone designated an apostle within the early Christian community, such as the author of the book of James.

2. Orthodoxy. Did the writing conform to the "rule of faith"? Scholars often use the Latin expression *regula fidei* when discussing this criterion, which refers to the practices and beliefs already accepted as normative for all Christians.
3. Catholicity. Did the writing have widespread use in Christian worship over a long period of time?

While there was some dispute over a few books, a high degree of consensus was achieved among diverse and geographically separated congregations. The book of Acts records an incident that may relate to the process of canonization. When the early Christian community had to practice group discernment about a growing number of Gentiles becoming Christians, the leaders met in Jerusalem. They debated whether these new believers should have to practice Jewish rituals as part of their newfound faith in Jesus. As the leaders of the church reached a decision to not unnecessarily burden new Gentile believers with Jewish practices, they prefaced their conclusions with the phrase "For it has seemed good to the Holy Spirit and to us" (Acts 15:28). In some ways, the process of canonization functioned similarly. Christian leaders concluded that twenty-seven of the writings that churches had already been using were what the Holy Spirit wanted; they would become what we call the New Testament.

THE CHALLENGE OF TRANSLATION

Imagine that the original Declaration of Independence of the United States was lost or destroyed. There would be no problem reconstructing the original, because many copies are extant and people have memorized the words. Also, the document isn't ancient (243 or so years is old but not ancient). Such reconstruction is similar but more complicated when it comes to the Bible. No original writings exist, because so much time has passed and the forerunner to paper easily disintegrated. However, there are numerous manuscripts of portions of the Bible, currently contained in libraries and museums, and copies of those are ubiquitous. Scholars painstakingly analyze these manuscripts in order to reconstruct the original documents.

There are an abundance of translations of the Bible into English and other modern languages, many of which are the result of careful study of a reconstructed original. Scholars are continually striving not only to identify the original words from the many manuscripts but also to give the sense of the original words in a way that modern readers can understand. For example, in the English-speaking world, the King James Version (KJV) has long been the most influential translation. It was produced in England in 1611. It strives to be a literal translation and was intended to reflect contemporary English, using the manuscripts known at the time.

Over the years, other English translations were developed based on manuscripts found after 1611. Typically, these translations attempt to reflect current English as well as target different reading levels. The New Revised Standard Version (NRSV) is popular among scholars, as it tends to be a literal rendering but also employs gender-inclusive language. The New International Version (NIV) attempts to give the sense of Scripture without always being literal, a process known as "dynamic equivalence." For example, consider 1 Corinthians 7:1 in these three versions:

KJV	NRSV	NIV
Now concerning the things whereof ye wrote unto me: It is good for a man not to touch a woman.	Now concerning the matters about which you wrote: "It is well for a man not to touch a woman."	Now for the matters you wrote about: "It is good for a man not to have sexual relations with a woman."

Notice how the KJV does not have quotation marks after the colon. Punctuation, such as quotation marks, was not part of the original Greek text. The more modern translations use quotation marks to show the issue that the apostle Paul is addressing in the chapter. Also, the KJV and the NRSV use the word *touch*, which is a literal translation of the Greek word in the text. The NIV, however, understands that *touch* is a euphemism and explains it with the phrase "have sexual relations."

There are so many English translations, and people often ask me, "Which one is the best?" It isn't always clear what the questioner means by "best," so it is hard to answer the question. For some, the best translation is the one that is most literal. For others, the best might be the one that is easiest to read. Still others might consider the best translation one that reflects a particular theological bias throughout.

It obviously isn't practical for everyone to study the ancient biblical languages, so I encourage the comparison of various translations when studying the Bible. It is not easy to capture the nuances of language in translations. Consider literary devices such as acrostics, assonance, and figures of speech, for example. We may fail to appreciate the creativity of the Bible, because such literary style is impossible to reproduce in a translation.

No matter where people land when choosing a translation, comparing translations reminds readers that the Bible did not originate in English. Doing the work of comparing helps to shed light on the way we might understand a Scripture passage. After all, we do want to get what the Bible has to say—to understand its purpose as best we can.

3

What Is the Center of the Bible?

Joe belonged to a church I attended several years ago. Perhaps you know someone like him. Joe (not his real name) regularly appeared at both morning and evening Sunday services, as well as at weekly Bible study and the men's monthly fellowship. On Sundays, he typically sat right in the center of a pew close to the front. During the sermon he would sometimes scowl at the pastor and flick through the pages of his Bible.

The pastor knew that Joe would be coming to argue with him at the end of the service. Joe always appeared grumpy and hardly ever talked about anything other than particular Bible verses. Once during a Bible study, when someone pondered aloud if Jesus had a sense of humor, Joe was adamant: Jesus was "too sober-minded and focused on his mission" for such things. We suspected that was also Joe's rationale for his own lack of humor.

Joe's frequent accusations that fellow church members were engaged in some egregious sin—or at least too tolerant of sin—made it hard for anyone to befriend him. I tried, as did several others. We learned that Joe was married and had adult children, but according to Joe, those relatives did not know Jesus. From the vantage point of years of pastoral experience, I can now imagine many reasons why Joe presented himself the way that he did. Perhaps his childhood was oppressive or even abusive. Maybe self-righteous behavior was modeled for him over many years. It could be that his faith in Jesus had allowed him to break an addiction, so that now only the most rigid expression of the faith could keep him sober. Who knows?

Even so, most of us who related to Joe back then felt that *loving* was not a word that would describe him. The associate pastor said to me that not only did adults try to avoid Joe, but so did little children. The pastor went on to wonder, "If children were comfortable around Jesus, how can Joe view himself as so Christlike when children try to avoid him?"

That associate pastor was applying a Christ-centered interpretation of Scripture. He was reasoning that the posture of Jesus toward children should be a model for us in our engagement with children. Also, the pastor was pointing out that a person's reading of the Bible, especially after many years, should result in that person becoming increasingly like Jesus.

Reading the Bible is not primarily about information but about transformation. The Bible helps us see Jesus as the heart of Christian faith, and it helps followers of Jesus develop Christlike character.

READING THE BIBLE BACKWARDS

The word *Christian* was an insult thrown in the faces of some of the earliest followers of Jesus Christ. Those believers were ostracized and criticized because they demonstrated allegiance to King Jesus. When they confessed that "Jesus is Lord," they were saying that Emperor Caesar was not. Furthermore, these believers in Jesus did not participate in the lewd activities that were part of life in the Roman Empire. Consequently, they faced ridicule and even persecution because of their abstinence. But followers of Jesus Christ wore the term *Christian* as a badge of honor rather than a shroud of shame. The apostle Peter encouraged: "Yet if any of you suffers as a Christian, do not consider it a disgrace, but glorify God because you bear this name" (1 Peter 4:16).

Jesus Christ has always been the center of faith and life for his followers, and Anabaptists were especially zealous in affirming the centrality of Jesus. During the Protestant Reformation of the sixteenth century, the Anabaptists' devotion to a Jesus-centered life put them at odds with other Reformers. Professor Stuart Murray points out that "for the Anabaptists, being Jesus-centered was a choice of ultimate loyalties, but the reformers seemed reluctant to risk the wrath of the political authorities by applying his teaching to social and economic issues."[1] Menno Simons, an early Anabaptist Reformer, wrote, "All the Scriptures, both the Old and the New Testaments, on every hand, point us to Christ Jesus that we are to follow him."[2]

Keeping Jesus at the center of faith not only means that he is the ultimate example of how we should live; it also means that he is the interpretive key to understanding the Bible. Jesus actually guides our interpretation of Scripture: "For Anabaptists, but not always for Christians in other traditions, this means that the Bible, as a record of what God has said and done in many generations, must be viewed through the prism of the revelation of God in Jesus Christ," writes Murray. "The Old Testament points forward to him; the New Testament points back to him."[3]

Reading the Bible in order to be like Jesus, and seeing Jesus as the interpretive key to Scripture, is referred to as Christ-centered hermeneutics, or **Christocentric hermeneutics**.

These passages in the New Testament are a few of the many that emphasize the uniqueness of Jesus and explain why he is central:

> No one has ever seen God. It is God the only Son, who is close to the Father's heart, who has made him known. (John 1:18)

> He is the image of the invisible God, the firstborn of all creation; for in him all things in heaven and on earth were created, things visible and invisible, whether thrones or dominions or rulers or powers—all things have been created through him and for him. He himself is before all things, and in him all things hold together. (Colossians 1:15-17)

> In the past God spoke to our ancestors through the prophets at many times and in various ways, but in these last days he has spoken to us by his Son, whom he appointed heir of all things, and through whom also he made the universe. The Son is the radiance of God's glory and the exact representation of his being, sustaining all things by his powerful word. After he had provided purification for sins, he sat down at the right hand of the Majesty in heaven. So he became as much superior to the angels as the name he has inherited is superior to theirs. (Hebrews 1:1-4 NIV)

Since Jesus, the Son, is the "exact representation" of God, the Father, we can understand more of the character of God by observing Jesus. The Gospels are a reliable record of what

Jesus said and did; familiarity with those writings is necessary for Christ-centered hermeneutics.

The Christ-centered approach to the Bible is multifaceted. That can be challenging—and perhaps frustrating—for those who prefer clear rules rather than principles and guidelines. Christocentric hermeneutics involves "reading backwards": finding Jesus in the Old Testament through images, people, prophecies, and events.[4] Those who read the Bible with Christ at the center understand Jesus as reenacting, as well as completing, Israel's history.

For example, Matthew uses the word *fulfill* to clearly connect Jesus to Israel (see Matthew 1:22; 2:15). When Jesus fasted in the wilderness for forty days and was tempted by Satan (Matthew 4:1-11), he was connecting to Israel's wandering in the wilderness for forty years. The Sermon on the Mount (Matthew 5–7) describes Jesus sitting on a mountainside to teach about devotion to God. That is reminiscent of Moses ascending Mount Sinai to receive the Ten Commandments (Exodus 19:1–20:17). Jesus is the fulfillment of Old Testament images, motifs, and prophecies. In Matthew 5:17, Jesus says, "Do not think that I have come to abolish the law or the prophets; I have come not to abolish but to fulfill." Jesus purports to be the culmination of what the Old Testament teaches.

A straightforward example comes from the book of Leviticus, whose lists of rituals can be confusing to contemporary readers. A key passage is Leviticus 16:1-34, which details the events involved in Yom Kippur, the Day of Atonement, when the high priest of the people of Israel performed rituals, including the sacrifice of animals, to atone for the sins of the nation. In the New Testament, the writer of Hebrews argues that the death of Jesus is the ultimate, once-for-all sacrifice, completing the picture outlined in Leviticus (see Hebrews 9:26). There are many more examples of how Jesus fulfills, or completes, the Old Testament.

In the example with Leviticus and Hebrews, the connection of Jesus to the Old Testament is explicit. However, employing Christocentric hermeneutics, or reading "backwards," may at times be less straightforward because of the lack of specific connection between the Old Testament and the New Testament. For example, Genesis 22:1-14 is a story known as the "binding of Isaac." My intent is not to explain the entire passage here but to make a point about reading backwards. In the story, God directs the patriarch Abraham to sacrifice his son Isaac: "After these things God tested Abraham. He said to him, 'Abraham!' And he said, 'Here I am.' He said, 'Take your son, your only son Isaac, whom you love, and go to the land of Moriah, and offer him there as a burnt offering on one of the mountains that I shall show you'" (Genesis 22:1-2).

Abraham moves out in obedience to God's direction, and Isaac assists in the preparations: "Abraham took the wood of the burnt offering and laid it on his son Isaac, and he himself carried the fire and the knife. So the two of them walked on together" (Genesis 22:6).

Jewish scholars of a later era, reflecting on the picture of Isaac carrying the wood intended to be used for his own death, compared it to Roman crucifixions when those being executed carried their own crosses. In the gospel of John, Jesus is said to have carried his own cross for his crucifixion (John 19:17). Without any explicit New Testament connection to Isaac in Genesis 22, many Christians view Isaac's actions as foreshadowing the crucifixion of Jesus. As seen in this case, the Christ-centered hermeneutic encourages readers to find resonance between events in the life of Jesus and Old Testament events or characters.

FLAT READING

A Christ-centered reading of the Bible is often placed in contrast to a "flat" reading of the Bible, in which every passage of Scripture is given equal emphasis.[5] Yet even readers who approach the Bible via a flat reading—typically people who speak of "following the whole Bible"—often choose for themselves which passages should carry more weight.

For example, some Christians say that capital punishment, a topic that is often hotly debated, is "required by the Bible." A flat reading of the Bible takes an Old Testament passage such as Genesis 9:6 and applies it to contemporary governments: "Whoever sheds the blood of a human, by a human shall that person's blood be shed; for in his own image God made humankind." But several pages later, in Exodus, the hero Moses murders an Egyptian overseer (Exodus 2:11-12). Moses was not executed, even though Genesis 9:6 suggests he should have been. In fact, God protects Moses from retribution and uses him powerfully to deliver Israel out of slavery.

Those who take a flat approach to the Bible may claim to read all of Scripture with equal emphasis, but in reality, they are selective about the application of particular verses. Capital punishment is not a mandate for all time in every place. A Christ-centered reading might consider the story of Jesus in John 8:1-11 as relevant to the topic of capital punishment. In that account, Jesus is confronted by a group of Jewish leaders who bring a woman allegedly caught in the act of adultery, an offense punishable by death according to Old Testament law. Jesus causes the woman's accusers to undertake some degree of self-reflection, and they soon depart, one after another. Jesus, standing and facing the woman, engages her in conversation: "'Woman, where are they? Has no one condemned you?' She said, 'No one, sir.' And Jesus said, 'Neither do I condemn you.

Go your way, and from now on do not sin again'" (vv. 10-11). The story clearly emphasizes forgiveness over punishment and should be considered when we think of what biblical justice might mean.

A Christocentric reading of Scripture not only pays attention to the historical and literary contexts of particular verses; it also involves the overarching story of the Bible with a focus on the way Jesus taught and acted. Christocentric hermeneutics means reading the Bible, including the Old Testament, with the goal of enhancing our love for God and others, because Jesus said that was the most important thing: "'You shall love the Lord your God with all your heart, and with all your soul, and with all your mind.' This is the greatest and first commandment. And a second is like it: 'You shall love your neighbor as yourself.' On these two commandments hang all the law and the prophets" (Matthew 22:37-40).

4

What Is the Spirit of the Bible?

During my college years as a chemical engineering student, I had a couple of opportunities to work in West Virginia at a large chemical company. The first time was over the course of a summer, a few months after my mother died of cancer. I lived on the campus of a small college and also attended a weekly Bible study, which was held in a nearby home and led by the pastor of a Presbyterian church. At the end of the summer, the pastor took me aside and asserted, "God wants you to give up engineering and go into ministry!" I was taken aback. I asked the pastor a bunch of questions, but I disagreed with his claim.

I went back to school, planning to be a chemical engineer, but I began struggling in the classroom. I returned to West Virginia to work again for several months, but I enjoyed little of my time there. After that second experience in West

Virginia, I went back to Ithaca, New York, to finish my studies at Cornell University. One Sunday morning, at the church that I and many other African American students attended near campus, I stood up before the congregation to ask for prayer. I was floundering emotionally. I had put lots of time, energy, and money into my engineering studies, but I was a mediocre student because I was a distracted student. My distractions related to my spiritual journey, to those times as an engineering intern in West Virginia, and to the death of my mother. I told the congregation that I thought maybe God was calling me into ministry, and they erupted with applause. They were already seeing something in my life that I needed to see.

God had spoken through the Presbyterian pastor, through circumstances in my life, through my church family, and through the Bible. In my heart I was hearing the words of Jesus spoken to the apostle Peter: "Feed my sheep" (John 21:17). Jesus was also calling me to feed his sheep. My experience is personal and subjective, but that is part of what it means to have Jesus at the center of life and to believe that he continues to speak to his people. Jesus promised to send the Holy Spirit to guide his followers (John 14:15-21; 15:26–16:15), and it is the Spirit who lives among God's people (1 Corinthians 3:16).

SPIRIT-LED HERMENEUTICS

The Holy Spirit speaks to us through the Bible, through circumstances, and through the fellowship of believers. God continues to speak so that the ancient words find meaning in present times. Peter describes God's Word as "living and enduring" (1 Peter 1:23), and the writer of Hebrews declares, "Indeed, the word of God is living and active, sharper than any two-edged sword, piercing until it divides soul from spirit,

joints from marrow; it is able to judge the thoughts and intentions of the heart" (Hebrews 4:12).

The Spirit of the Bible is the Holy Spirit, who was behind
the writing of the Bible and is active in the interpretation and
application of the Bible's story. "All scripture is inspired by
God," claims 2 Timothy 3:16. The word translated "inspired"
is literally "God-breathed," which in the Greek is *theopneus-
tos*. A related Greek word is *pneuma*, translated as "spirit,"
"wind," or "breath." Thus, 2 Timothy 3:16 connects the Holy
Spirit to the production of the Old Testament: the breath, or
Spirit, of God was at work in human beings, who took the stories that were passed along and wrote the words onto pages.
In 2 Peter 1:20-21, the author asserts: "First of all you must
understand this, that no prophecy of scripture is a matter of
one's own interpretation, because no prophecy ever came by
human will, but men and women moved by the Holy Spirit
spoke from God."[1]

The Holy Spirit worked through human beings to write the
Bible, and the Holy Spirit still works through human beings
to interpret the Bible. Biblical scholar Joel Green asserts, "As
the Spirit of Christ was active in the generation of Scriptures,
so, in our actualization of the Scriptures the Spirit points us
to Christ."[2] A similar line of thinking is behind what biblical
scholar Craig Keener refers to as "Spirit hermeneutics," which
includes relying on the Holy Spirit to aid in our understanding
and application of biblical texts.[3]

Early Anabaptists were of the same mind as Green and
Keener. In the sixteenth century, Peter Riedeman wrote, "As the
scripture came by the Holy Spirit we must let it be judged by
the same. Who, however, can attain this judgment apart from
man who hath the Holy Spirit, for the carnal man receiveth
not the things of the Spirit of God."[4] Riedeman wrote with

1 Corinthians 2:14 in view: "But the natural man receiveth not the things of the Spirit of God: for they are foolishness unto him: neither can he know them, because they are spiritually discerned" (KJV).

WHAT DIFFERENCE DOES THE SPIRIT MAKE?

Dependence upon the Holy Spirit in biblical interpretation acknowledges that those without formal education can understand the Word of God and apply it to real-life situations. Such was the case when African American slaves were prevented from learning to read. Yet they still managed not only to respect the Bible but to find hope within the words of Scripture that they heard.

During the Protestant Reformation, there was increasing emphasis on the need for formal education in order to interpret the Scriptures. Early Anabaptists clashed with others in the Reformation movement in that Anabaptists believed ordinary Christians, lacking formal theological training, could responsibly interpret the Bible. The community of God's people possess the Spirit of God, since they have placed their faith in Jesus, and the community of God is thus empowered to interpret the Scriptures.

Reliance on the Holy Spirit, however, does not devalue the gift of scholarship. As Craig Keener points out, "Scripture by virtue of its textual form must be approached in the sorts of ways in which we must approach texts."[5] Biblical texts must be studied, and we can study them ourselves and also listen to scholars, who help us pay attention to Scripture's ancient as well as contemporary contexts.

I often tell congregants and students, "The Holy Spirit does not bless laziness." What I mean is that diligent study is part of our task. The apostle Paul gave this admonition to his protégé

Timothy: "Do your best to present yourself to God as one approved by him, a worker who has no need to be ashamed, rightly explaining the word of truth" (2 Timothy 2:15). Doing one's best means giving serious energy and attention to the task. Illumination by the Holy Spirit does not excuse us from doing the work of **exegesis**: drawing out the meaning of a text. The Bible was first written by and to people who lived long before us. We are separated from the original hearers and readers by time and culture, which includes language, customs, and perceptions of the universe—including all dimensions of scientific understanding. Therefore, faithfully approaching Scripture means doing our best to get some sense of what the first hearers or readers might have understood the various passages in the Bible to be saying. (We'll look at this more in chapter 5).

In addition to diligent study, we rely on the Holy Spirit for guidance. Theologian Donald Bloesch puts it like this: "The Bible is not rightly understood when it is treated primarily as a collection of texts amenable to historical analysis and dissection. It is certainly a historical document but it is much more than that. Its worthiness as a theological guide and norm does not become clear until it is acclaimed as the sword of the Spirit (Eph 6:17), the divinely chosen instrument by which the powers of sin and death are overthrown in the lives of those who believe."[6]

Some people are hesitant to affirm Spirit-led hermeneutics, imagining it to be a subjective and speculative enterprise. Doesn't an emphasis on Spirit-led reading of Scripture make interpretation vulnerable to the whims and circumstances of the interpreter? The early Anabaptists of the sixteenth century recognized the problem of personal perspectives guiding interpretation. Menno Simons, an Anabaptist leader in the Netherlands from whom the Mennonites take their name, urged that "reason be used to check against wild interpretations."[7]

The Scriptures had meaning before we showed up, and they will continue to have meaning after we're gone. We interpret them as faithfully as we can, and depend on the Holy Spirit to guide our interpretation. On one hand, we do not determine the meaning of Scripture on our own, finding new or avant-garde meanings of Bible verses. On the other hand, approaching the Bible with only reason, and as merely an ancient document, ignores the work of the Holy Spirit. Doing analytic work on the Bible can uncover helpful information, such as the use of language and the way ancient culture operated, but won't necessarily connect anyone to God in any significant way. We need the Spirit, working within our reason, our imagination, and our community, to help us.

Consider, for example, a painful topic that has ramifications for our current times: slavery. Slavery has been practiced throughout human history, and is prominent in both the Old and New Testaments. In fact, there are commands directed at Christian slaves in the New Testament. Ephesians 6:5-6 says, "Slaves, obey your earthly masters with fear and trembling, in singleness of heart, as you obey Christ; not only while being watched, and in order to please them, but as slaves of Christ, doing the will of God from the heart." And these words from 1 Peter 2:18 are especially difficult for many contemporary Bible readers: "Slaves, accept the authority of your masters with all deference, not only those who are kind and gentle but also those who are harsh."

Interpreting these verses about slavery requires that we pay attention to the lessons that we have learned over time about the evils of the institution; that we appreciate the way

Jesus taught and acted; and that we notice how the Holy Spirit has been at work in Christian community over the years. The Holy Spirit shows us that it would be wrong to conclude that Jesus endorses the cruelty of slavery. Even though there are no explicit condemnations of slavery in the Bible, the more we understand about Jesus, the less we can tolerate oppression and injustice, such as slavery. Our rejection of injustice is fruit of the work of the Holy Spirit.

THE AUTHORITY OF THE BIBLE

It is the Spirit of God that gives the Bible its authority. Sometimes people speak of the "authority of Scripture" in the way that my old acquaintance Joe did: They focus on the words almost to the exclusion of the Person behind the words. They act as if the Bible's authority means that saying a verse (or shouting it) will make its meaning clearer and more relevant, and will cause other people to change. God wields authority in a different way than we might expect. Biblical scholar N. T. Wright says, "God's authority vested in scripture is designed, as all God's authority is designed, to liberate human beings, to judge and condemn evil and sin in the world in order to set people free to be fully human. That's what God is in the business of doing. That is what his authority is there *for*. And when we use a shorthand phrase like 'authority of scripture' that is what we ought to be meaning. It is an authority with this shape and character, this purpose and goal."[8]

The Bible's authority is *derived*; that is, it gets its authority from God, who is Father, Son, and Holy Spirit. I noted in the previous chapter that the Bible centers on Jesus. After his resurrection, Jesus told his closest followers that "all authority in heaven and on earth has been given to me" (Matthew 28:18). The voice of Jesus is authoritative; we must listen to him (Matthew 17:5). Since Jesus speaks through the Bible, its authority comes from him.

Several Protestant denominations and seminaries refer to the Bible's authority in matters of faith and life. Here are a few examples:

- Mennonite World Conference: "As a faith community, we accept the Bible as our authority for faith and life."

- Northern Seminary (where I teach): "We submit to the authority of the Word of God, incarnate in Jesus Christ, made known in the whole of scripture as the supreme authority for faith and practice."

- Fuller Seminary (a well-known and respected institution): "Scripture is an essential part and trustworthy record of this divine self-disclosure. All the books of the Old and New Testaments, given by divine inspiration, are the written Word of God, the only infallible rule of faith and practice. They are to be interpreted according to their context and purpose and in reverent obedience to the Lord who speaks through them in living power."

- The Evangelical Covenant Church (which holds my ordination credentials): "We affirm the centrality of the word of God. We believe the Bible is the only perfect rule for faith, doctrine, and conduct. The dynamic, transforming power of the word of God directs the church and the life of each Christian."

These Christians recognize that the Bible is not a mathematics or science textbook, or even a comprehensive history book. The Bible guides its readers to be more like Jesus.

The Spirit of the Bible is the same Spirit who lives within and among God's people, so we can be confident that God will not lead astray those who truly seek to follow Jesus. Anabaptist leader Pilgram Marpeck wrote in 1542, "We would certainly admonish every Christian to be on the alert and personally to study the Scriptures, and have a care lest he permit himself to be easily moved and led away from Scripture and apostolic doctrine by strange teaching and understanding. But let everyone, according to Scripture and apostolic teaching, strive with great diligence to do God's will, seeing that the Word of Truth could not fail us nor mislead us."[9]

On a practical level, the best study of the Bible involves our heads, hearts, and hands. The best reading of Scripture occurs when we, together, perform detailed study of the ancient text, accompanied by prayer for the Spirit's guidance and for help to obey what we are learning.

5

Who Gets to Interpret the Bible?

Years ago I came across a cartoon that made me burst out laughing. The cartoon pictured three people sitting in a semicircle and dressed in what appeared to be first-century attire. One person held a scroll and had his mouth open to speak. The heading at the top of the cartoon announced: "Bible Study, AD 75." The caption quoted the one holding the scroll: "I believe Paul wants us all to go around and say what this verse means to you."

Doesn't that capture virtually every church or home Bible study group you've attended? For me it does. As a pastor and instructor of the Bible for many years, I frequently show the cartoon to church laity and seminary students. I've observed how reactions differ. Older people tend to laugh with familiarity, as I had done, because they doubt the apostle Paul would invite others to bring their meaning to his writing.

But younger people tend not to laugh at the cartoon. Many like the cartoon, but they don't find it humorous. Younger Bible readers typically *expect* to exercise power and freedom in biblical interpretation. As one of my students said of the cartoon, "I like that people are invited to discuss the text." That student had come from a church background where congregants were encouraged not to engage the biblical text but merely to receive authoritative teaching from the priest or pastor.

One goal of the Protestant Reformation was to help ordinary people read and understand the Bible. Consider that Martin Luther developed a translation of the entire Bible—from Hebrew, Aramaic, and Greek—so that literate German Christians could read it for themselves and not have to rely on clergy to tell them what the Bible says. One reason slave owners in the New World criminalized the education of slaves was that they knew that education is power, and that reading the Bible is especially empowering. As scholar Barbara E. Reid declares, "Interpreting the Bible is an act of power."[1]

THE BIBLE SAYS IT. DOES THAT SETTLE IT?

We all read texts, including the Bible, with a set of lenses that color our understanding of the passages we read. Our place in society, our gender, our ethnic background, and a host of other factors contribute to our understanding of any given text. Scholars use the term *social location* to refer to the reader's background. Because our social locations vary, we bring differing personal assumptions and aspirations to our understanding of Scripture passages. Consequently, we cannot help but interpret the Scriptures while we read them. It is not possible to simply read the Bible—or any text—without supplying some sort of interpretation.

Some people claim to read the Bible plainly, or clearly, without interpreting it. They might even say, "I just do what the Bible says." Those who take such a position rely heavily on assumptions behind **inerrancy**: a belief that the Bible contains no contradictions and no historical or scientific inaccuracies. This term has often been used in discussions of the Bible. Those with this view of inerrancy understand contradictions and inaccuracies to be lies, and since it is impossible for God to lie (Hebrews 6:18), the Bible, as God's Word, must be inerrant. With that perspective, readers may think that the way they read the Scriptures is free from any interpretative bias. For example, in the sixteenth century, the astronomer Nicolaus Copernicus concluded that the earth revolves around the sun, not the other way around. But Christians—both Roman Catholics as well as members of the new Protestant movement—rejected the views of Copernicus, partly based on their understanding of biblical passages, such as Joshua 10:12-13, which describes the sun as standing still. Current debates include issues related to the origins of the universe. For some Bible readers, holding to a strict notion of inerrancy means the creation story of Genesis 1 must be taken literally. This puts those readers at odds with vast amounts of scientific findings.

The common concept of inerrancy is too confining; it limits contemporary understanding of the Scriptures. We know today that slavery is wrong, even though the Bible does not explicitly condemn it. A strict view of inerrancy might lead some to conclude that the apostle Paul's admonition for slaves to "obey your earthly masters in everything" (Colossians 3:22) is a command for all times. Sadly, history has shown that some people's readings of the Bible have led to the creation of oppressive institutions that contradict the way of Jesus. Professors Grace Ji-Sun Kim and Susan M. Shaw point out that "the Bible plays a key role in either reinforcing the status quo or prompting action toward liberation."[2]

Some scholars prefer the term **infallibility** in describing the Bible. This term is different from inerrancy in that it suggests that the Bible, when faithfully read, does not deceive or lead to spiritual error. Infallibility recognizes the imperfect human element in the writing of Scripture and simultaneously affirms the Holy Spirit's authority to communicate God and God's intentions for the world.

FINDING THE MEANING OF SCRIPTURE THROUGH COMMUNITY

The power of biblical interpretation is best experienced in the context of church community. Peter J. Gomes describes the Bible as "a public record" of the relationship between people and God: "When we realize the oral origins of scripture, and the fact that in the days before general literacy the only way that people became acquainted with the Bible was to hear it in the company of others, read aloud by one who could do so, then we realize that like the ancient tales of Homer and the histories of Greece and Rome these were public stories that communicated public truths in the most public of ways."[3]

The early Anabaptists employed what is known as **congregational hermeneutics**: the practice of interpreting the Bible by respecting and affirming the presence of the Holy Spirit in the lives of all believers. The Anabaptists represented one part of the Protestant Reformation, and they were in accord with other Reformers in rejecting the Roman Catholic practice of the time of having clergy (priests and theologians) be the only ones who could interpret Scripture. But the Anabaptists veered from other Reformers in some ways. For some within the Protestant Reformation, the goal of biblical study was to find the correct, authoritative interpretation, and they assumed scholars were best suited for such an enterprise. The spiritual descendants of these Reformers today still engage in the same practice, offering edicts and statements designed to give the definite word on particular topics within Scripture.

Anabaptists advocated congregational hermeneutics, in which the meaning of Scripture is discerned by churches reading and praying together. Congregational hermeneutics includes more, however, than just a lone contemporary congregation deciding for itself what the Bible means. In congregational hermeneutics, *community* needs to be defined as 1) including both ancient and contemporary believers; 2) including those who are formally trained as well as those who are not; and 3) centering those who have historically been marginalized or ignored. Let's consider the reasons these three elements of congregational hermeneutics are important.

COMMUNITY OF THE PAST

Christians sometimes refer to Hebrews 11 as the "Hall of Faith" because it is replete with examples of people from the Old Testament who lived "by faith." (An interesting exercise is to go through that chapter and count the frequent rhetorical use of the phrase "by faith"). Hebrews 12:1 calls the heroes referenced in Hebrews 11 a great "cloud of witnesses." Innumerable people who lived in bygone eras had tremendous faith in God, and we should learn from them and be motivated by them. We can always learn from those who preceded us in the faith.

For example, the early church father Athanasius of Alexandria (AD 296–373) wrote a well-respected analysis of the Psalms. In his reflection, Athanasius points out how the book of Psalms encompasses the teaching of the other Bible books in that it "contains in itself what is found in all of them, like a garden, and expresses them in song."[4] Centuries later, Martin Luther would describe the Psalms similarly, as "a little Bible." Athanasius also described the therapeutic role that the psalms play, encouraging anyone who hears them to learn "what one must say and do to heal one's disordered feelings."[5]

As contemporary readers, we can confirm that much of the teaching of other parts of the Bible are found in the Psalms. By experience, we who love the psalms know that, as poetry, they speak to our emotions as well as our intellect. The sense we make of Psalms, shared with these earlier readers, is a good reminder that many of the readings of our forebears in the faith are insightful and fruitful. We should never assume that the only valid biblical interpretations are the products of contemporary study and reflection.

It is, of course, impossible to consult every word on every biblical text, but at least some effort should be made to engage the Christian community of the past. Much present-day scholarship interacts not only with the writers of a few generations ago but also with ancient scholars from the early centuries of Christian faith whose writings still survive. At the same time, we must acknowledge the reality that contemporary scholarship—with its attention to other disciplines, such as archaeology and social sciences—yields fresh insights into the Scriptures.

COMMUNITY OF THE TRAINED AND THE UNTRAINED

Reading and otherwise engaging the work of biblical scholars is part of congregational hermeneutics. Sadly, many Christians hold an anti-intellectual bias. I can't count how many times I've heard the purposeful slip of the tongue when someone refers to "seminary" as "cemetery." The assumption is that formal education kills vibrant faith.

There is no question that some people have reconsidered aspects of their faith as a result of formal study, and others have abandoned Christianity altogether. But as with most matters, there is always much more below the surface. People's reasons for abandoning their faith are not entirely intellectual. Seminary and other avenues of formal study have helped multitudes of Christians become more knowledgeable of the Bible, more confident in teaching as well as living it. The path toward biblical interpretation passes through history, runs alongside the work of those privileged to study formally, and comes right up to those who are asking, "So what?"

CENTERING THE MARGINALIZED

The Bible was written by and to people who were marginalized. Faithful readers of Scripture recognize that the believing community includes those who have historically been marginalized or ignored. Congregational hermeneutics requires that readers be willing to read as part of groups that are economically, racially, sexually, and otherwise diverse.

Among my fondest memories of being a pastor are the conversations and actions that happened in a congregational Bible study. At times we read or cited biblical commentaries and engaged the original Hebrew or Greek language of a passage in the Bible. Often, however, we listened to and affirmed the observations and insights of people with very little formal education of any kind. People whose faith is deep, often refined in the furnace of suffering, bring well-earned insight to the Scriptures.

The storytellers, writers, and first readers of the Bible—both testaments—were, for the most part, people of low status in society. Faithful interpretation of the Bible today requires reckoning with this truth. With regard to the Old Testament, Israel was a small player on the world stage (Deuteronomy 7:7). As for the New Testament, the first-century Christian community was initially viewed as a sect within Judaism and functioned under the oppressive Roman Empire. Furthermore, the Bible exhibits a consistent theme of God working through those who are unlikely candidates—people of low status, including women and slaves.

We who long to get a clearer sense of what is happening in the Bible must receive with humility the perspectives that historically marginalized people bring. The interpretation of Scripture by Christian women, along with believers who are non-white and non-Western, has often been ignored.[6] Consider, for example, that the so-called Bible Belt of the United States has been the location of some of the most brazen displays of white supremacy and horrendous acts of brutality, such as lynching. Interpreting the Bible privately, or even in groups that do not reflect the diversity of God's kingdom, can result in false assumptions and possibly even violence. Megalomaniacs and cult leaders, like the infamous Jim Jones of the People's Temple, arise periodically and are sober reminders of the danger of elevating private interpretations of the Bible.

HOW DO WE DO IT?

One question that emerges right away is a practical one: How might we study the Bible in community, especially when most churches focus on weekend worship events that include a sermon whose message is likely the only Scripture teaching most people will receive? As a pastor, I often encouraged discussion of the sermon in weekly Bible studies. Of course, that requires that people attend gatherings outside of Sunday services. I'm aware that some Anabaptist congregations practice a form of engagement with Scripture teaching called *zeugnis* (German for "testimony"). In a friend's church, *zeugnis* involves passing around a microphone so that anyone can share insights and responses to the sermon.

Over the years I've grown in my respect and admiration for the role of small groups, having experienced them well before I became a pastor and then all throughout my pastoral ministry. Much of North American Christianity seems to measure success in the number of people who attend weekend worship services but downplay the importance of smaller gatherings. The pastors who garner the most praise as well as speaking engagements are those who attract large numbers of bodies and dollars at worship services. However, there is a favorable image of the early church that we get in Acts 2:42-47 that needs our constant attention:

> They devoted themselves to the apostles' teaching and fellowship, to the breaking of bread and the prayers. Awe came upon everyone, because many wonders and signs were being done by the apostles. All who believed were together and had all things in common; they would sell their possessions and goods and distribute the proceeds to all, as any had need. Day by day, as they spent much time together in the temple, they broke bread at home and ate their food with glad and generous hearts, praising God and having the goodwill of all the people. And day by day the Lord added to their number those who were being saved.

Granted, the passage does follow from the acknowledgment that more than three thousand people came to believe in Jesus on a holiday called Pentecost. However, the description here is not about how a large worship service took place. Instead, the emphasis is on more intimate gatherings. The mutual concern described in the passage—as well as the learning, the sharing of meals, and the experience of spiritually powerful events—is best replicated in small groups that might flow out of larger gatherings. The early followers of Jesus in Jerusalem attended the temple there, but they also met in homes. Small groups allow for personal connections. To the point of this chapter, small groups are the best atmosphere for congregational hermeneutics, because smaller groups allow for discussion and discernment. Food can often serve as a social lubricant, helping minimize friction among members, because tensions sometimes arise when discussing the meaning of Scripture passages.

The practice of congregational hermeneutics may look different in different settings. It may require creativity, imagination, and the willingness to break with some traditions. Wisdom dictates that Christians practice some form of congregational hermeneutics in a diverse setting. "Where there is no guidance, a nation falls, but in an abundance of counselors there is safety" (Proverbs 11:14).

6

What Impact Does the Bible Make?

The Bible is not a magic book. You may have seen movies like those based on the Harry Potter series, in which characters recite spells and immediately people are frozen in their tracks, or inanimate objects come to life, or there's a snowstorm in summer. Just by someone saying the correct words in the proper way, the laws of nature are suspended. Oftentimes we don't even see a supernatural being behind the recitation of a spell; the words themselves appear to contain all the power and authority.

Even though God's Word is described as "living and active" (Hebrews 4:12), the Bible is not a book of incantations. Yet sometimes Christians read the Bible as if it were such a book. They behave as if they can simply read the words—sometimes noting that there must be a proper attitude or correct amount of faith—and then circumstances will change. People who view the Bible as a magic book tend to fixate on its words, but they run the risk of devaluing the God whom the words are about. When people act as if the Bible were a collection of verses to be quoted at random and applied to particular situations, they might miss the likelihood that God wants to change *them*, even if their circumstances remain the same.

In the introduction, we noted that there can be negative—even violent—impacts when people read the Bible in certain ways. Those faulty readings result from failing to acknowledge that the center of the Bible is Jesus, failing to discern the Spirit of the Bible, and failing to practice interpreting the Bible with a diverse community of other Jesus-followers. God intends for the Bible to have a positive impact, which is the development of people who love God and love others. The goals of Scripture study include growing in the grace and knowledge of the Lord and Savior Jesus Christ (2 Peter 3:18); taking on the righteous character of Jesus (2 Timothy 3:16); and being equipped to teach others (2 Timothy 2:15). In essence, the goal of reading Scripture is to *embody* Scripture, not just individually but as part of Christian community.

OBEDIENCE TO CHRIST, TOGETHER

Embodying Scripture means being obedient to it. Anabaptists stress obedience as necessary for the study of Scripture. "The readiness to obey Christ's words is prerequisite to understanding them," writes one Anabaptist theologian. "All the sophistication of interpretive methodology will be of no avail if the reader and interpreter of Scripture is not ready to obey Christ's words in his life."[1] Not only is obedience a prerequisite; for those who would follow Jesus, obedience to Christ is also the goal of Scripture study.

I stress that there needs to be *corporate* and not just *individual* embodiment of Scripture. After all, the writings of the Bible were intended for communities of people. Even works initially addressed to individuals—such as Philemon, 1 & 2 Timothy, and Titus—were read aloud for the entire Christian community. They were copied and shared.

Given the highly individualistic nature of Western society, it might be difficult for us to even imagine an answer to the question, What does it mean to embody Scripture as a community? We are so accustomed to thinking about what it means for *me* to follow Jesus or for *you* to obey Scripture. We may have a hard time imagining what it means for *us* to obey the Word of God together.

Let's consider Philippians 1:6 as an example. One translation reads: "And I am sure of this, that he who began a good work in you will bring it to completion at the day of Jesus Christ" (ESV). That translation is typical of most English versions. But consider another translation: "I am confident of this, that the one who began a good work among you will bring it to completion by the day of Jesus Christ" (NRSV). Notice how the ESV has "*in* you" and the NRSV has "*among* you," which captures that the "you" is actually the plural form in Greek.

When most people in the West hear the "in you" translation, they likely hear an individual promise. I certainly heard it that way during most of my years in the church. Philippians 1:6 is typically preached in a way to assure individuals that God will bring them to maturity in the faith. The NRSV translation, however, with "among," highlights that the "you" is plural in the Greek text. It is quite possible that the apostle Paul's confidence is related to the communal spiritual progress of the Christians in Philippi.

When we keep in mind that many of the words in the Bible translated "you" are plural and not singular, it will change how we hear much of Scripture. Writers of Scripture typically had an entire community of people in mind. Consider another letter from the apostle Paul, 2 Corinthians. The apostle commends the entire community, suggesting that they can vouch for his character: "Surely we do not need, as some do, letters of recommendation to you or from you, do we? You yourselves are our letter, written on our hearts, to be known and read by all; and you show that you are a letter of Christ, prepared by us, written not with ink but with the Spirit of the living God, not on tablets of stone but on tablets of human hearts" (2 Corinthians 3:1-3).

When Paul refers to the Corinthian Christians as "letters" that are "known and read by all," he is saying that the community of believers embody what Paul has taught them. They can vouch for Paul's ministry because it has taken root, by the power of the Holy Spirit. We become aware of God's salvation—announced as "good news," the meaning of the word *gospel*—partly through reading the Scriptures (Romans 10:17). That salvation must be modeled by Christian communities. In one of his several studies of the apostle Paul, biblical scholar Michael J. Gorman argues that "the gospel must become flesh and blood in and as the church. Which is to say as well that the church must become the gospel, embodying God's salvation."[2]

Jesus did not present himself in the manner of some ancient religious leaders who separated themselves from other people. Some cultures had prophets, or oracles, who lived apart from the society, requiring people to make a pilgrimage to hear the oracle's pronouncements. Jesus was the opposite. He chose to make his home among people (John 1:14). Jesus even developed close friendships (see John 11:3; 15:13-15). Jesus demonstrated the importance of community by the way he lived. His followers communicate to the rest of the world that Jesus is still alive and active by the way they lovingly relate to each other (see John 13:34-35). We embody the gospel of Jesus when we strive to live together in love.

A STRATEGY FOR UNDERSTANDING THE BIBLE

During my thirty years of pastoring, I noticed that increasing numbers of people mistrust churches and denominations. Some distrust seems to be based on the many celebrity pastors who cheat people out of their money, lie about immoral behavior, or otherwise abuse their power and position. Such was the case several years ago when popular televangelist Jim Bakker was indicted on federal charges of mail and wire fraud, and of conspiring to defraud the public. It was also revealed that he had an adulterous relationship with a church secretary, who accused him of raping her. (Bakker denied the allegations.) Bakker, originally sentenced to forty-five years in prison, served eight years. Although he wrote a book entitled *I Was Wrong*, Bakker returned to televangelism and has continued to make controversial pronouncements.

More recently, well-known pastor Mark Driscoll left Mars Hill Church after controversy surrounding his alleged domineering style of leadership. In 2018, the widely influential pastor Bill Hybels, founder of Willow Creek Community Church, resigned six months earlier than his anticipated retirement when allegations of sexual misconduct were made against him after over four decades of ministry.

Adding insult to injury is the frequent failure of church structures to address issues of abuse. Both the Roman Catholic Church and the largest American Protestant denomination, the Southern Baptist Convention, covered up years of sexual abuse perpetrated by clergy. The skepticism of some may not be entirely justified, but to the degree that it is, churches would do well to keep in mind that the study of Scripture is not so much about being right as about being good. And by "good" I mean "like Jesus." Yes, the Word of God is a sword of the Spirit, discharged to combat evil (Ephesians 6:17; Hebrews 4:12), but it is not meant to be a weapon used to dehumanize, degrade, or otherwise damage people. People are not the enemy (Ephesians 6:12).

Experiencing the positive impact of the Bible presumes thoughtful engagement with it. As we come to the end of the book, let's look at five elements of a basic strategy for exegesis and hermeneutics—which is to say, understanding, interpreting, and enacting the Scriptures.

1. Be a humble, prayerful, collegial learner. Individual study is good, and being personally invested in the prayerful reading of Scripture can be transformative. Be ready to bring what you are observing during your own reading of Scripture into a group context. Be willing to be shaped and corrected by group discussion, as well as by other interpersonal interactions. Expect the Holy Spirit to communicate in some way through the group experience. Also keep in mind that part of what it means to be collegial is paying attention to how others have understood particular biblical passages. Read ancient as well as contemporary commentary on Scripture, being careful to include the voices of women and others on the margins of society.

2. Pay attention to the genre of a particular biblical passage. If I start a sentence with "A priest, a rabbi, and a minister went into a bar," you'd rightly suspect that I was telling a joke. Jokes are potentially absurd and are expected to have a punch line. Likewise, opening with "Once upon a time" suggests I'm telling a fairy tale. In that case, animals might talk, frogs could turn into princes, the laws of nature may be suspended, and the heroes live "happily ever after."

My point is that genre contributes to our understanding of how texts operate. The Bible contains narratives, poems, parables, letters, and a variety of other literary genres that are often connected to oral forms, like jokes and fairy tales are. Consider this poetic passage from Isaiah 55:12: "For you shall go out in joy, and be led back in peace; the mountains and the hills before you shall burst into song, and all the trees of the field shall clap their hands." Mountains and hills do not possess vocal cords, and trees do not have hands. Those who claim to take the Bible literally have a challenge with this verse and others like it. Respecting that the verse is poetic means letting the images speak to us in addition to the words. Poetry, perhaps more than other genres, is intended to stimulate our emotions and imaginations, not just convey information.

3. Respect context. By "context" I mean both the literary context and the historical context of the passage. The literary context is how a particular passage fits into the entire book. For example, when the apostle Paul writes, "I can do all things through him who strengthens me" (Philippians 4:13), he is not making a blanket statement that would allow him to, say, jump off a cliff and not get hurt. It is not a statement declaring that any random thing at all can be accomplished with God's strength. In the context, Paul refers to having his material needs met so he can carry out his ministry. The previous verse (Philippians 4:12) says, "I know what it is to have little, and I know what it is to have plenty. In any and all circumstances I have learned the secret of being well-fed and of going hungry, of having plenty and of being in need." Paul is saying that God strengthened or sustained him—materially—so that he could accomplish all that he was called to do.

Along with the literary context is the historical one. An example might be 2 John 9-11: "Everyone who does not abide in the teaching of Christ, but goes beyond it, does not have God; whoever abides in the teaching has both the Father and the Son. Do not receive into the house or welcome anyone who comes to you and does not bring this teaching; for to welcome is to participate in the evil deeds of such a person."

The passage warns against welcoming false teachers. Some contemporary Christians have thought that the word *house* in the passage refers to private homes, so they have been wary of any unbelievers coming into their residence, even to the point of seeking out only Christian plumbers or other tradespeople. A study of the historical context reveals that "house" refers to the meeting place of the Christian community. The passage warns against false teachers developing a role within the Christian community. It is helpful to consult a few of the many scholarly commentaries that shed light on literary and historical contexts.

4. Consider how your contemporary situation might mirror the situation in the Scripture text. For example, many of the stories in the Gospels reference peasants in an agrarian society, while many readers in the modern West might, like me, be urban dwellers. I've never been responsible for sheep, but when I read in Matthew 9:36 that "when he [Jesus] saw the crowds, he had compassion for them, because they were harassed and helpless, like sheep without a shepherd," I can appreciate the point. I've encountered plenty of beleaguered and rudderless people in my years of urban ministry. I understand that my disposition toward "harassed and helpless" people must be one not of judgment but of compassion.

5. Ask questions of the text that keep the bigger story, as well as your place in that story, in mind. Here are some good questions to ask as you read:

- What might the passage say about God (Father, Son, and Holy Spirit)?
- What might the passage say about people?
- How might the passage be inviting us to be more like Jesus (in the way we think or behave)?

These five guidelines are not meant to be exclusive or exhaustive. They can, however, get us off to a great start in our study of the Scriptures.

LETTING THE WORD OF CHRIST FIND A HOME

The Holy Scriptures help us center our lives on Jesus Christ so that we can be whole people: those whose bodies and souls are nourished through receiving and sharing the love of God among the people of God. In the last two chapters of the letter to the Colossians, we find several practical admonitions for the church community, starting at Colossians 3:1. In order to experience healthy community life, several virtues, such as compassion, kindness, humility, meekness, and patience, must be present (see Colossians 3:12). There must be a willingness to forgive (v. 13). Love must be central (v. 14). The peace of Christ needs to permeate the grateful community (v. 15). And it is the word of Christ that motivates the Christian community by provoking our minds and our hearts.

Colossians 3:16 reads, "Let the word of Christ dwell in you richly; teach and admonish one another in all wisdom; and with gratitude in your hearts sing psalms, hymns, and spiritual songs to God." Words *from* Christ and words *about* Christ—which are both found primarily in the Bible—must find a home among the Christian community.

To *dwell* means to find a home, and that image evokes feelings of welcome, warmth, and comfort. This word of Christ must find a home *richly*, or *abundantly*. When the word of

Christ finds a home among God's people, it gets treated as more than a guest who visits from time to time; it settles in, is treated with respect, and is given time and attention, just like any other member of the family.

The word of Christ will influence our communication as we teach and admonish one another, as well as when we sing together. I say that the word of Christ provokes our minds because teaching and admonition affect how we think so that our behaviors change for the better. Even the virtues I pointed out from the previous verses are reinforced through the teaching and admonition of the word of Christ. Notice that teaching and admonition are mutual; they happen between one another, not just from one person to a crowd. Teaching and admonition accompany singing, which typically stimulates our emotions. Psalms, hymns, and spiritual songs may urge us to lament as well as celebrate, to grieve as well as praise.

When the word of Christ is allowed to find a home among the people of God, it will lead to healthy interpersonal dynamics, which in turn will communicate God's presence to the onlooking world. Many will see that the followers of Jesus—those who let the word of Christ find a home among them—are those who make space for God to work. We who let the word of Christ dwell among us anticipate that God brings deliverance to those who are bound, freedom for those who recognize Jesus Christ is king, and transformation for all of God's creation.

Glossary

apocalyptic writing: A style of writing in which an individual is granted insights into other-worldly mysteries accompanied by an angelic being. Apocalyptic writing has many stylistic tropes, such as symbolic numbers, symbolic personae, and portents of a cataclysmic battle between good and evil.

Apocrypha: The fifteen writings included in the Greek Old Testament (Septuagint), written about two hundred years before the New Testament: Tobit, Judith, Esther (Greek version), Wisdom of Solomon, Sirach (also known as Ecclesiasticus, or the Wisdom of Ben Sira), Baruch, Letter of Jeremiah, Prayer of Azariah and the Song of the Three Jews (from the book of Daniel), Susanna (connected to the Greek book of Daniel), Bel and the Dragon (also connected to Daniel), 1 & 2 Maccabees, 1 Esdras, Prayer of Manasseh, 2 Esdras. These writings are considered canonical by the Orthodox Church and deuterocanonical by the Roman Catholic Church.

Christocentric hermeneutics: The perspective that Jesus Christ is the center of Scripture and both testaments point to him in some way. Therefore, our interpretation of the Bible takes both the character and teachings of Jesus into account. Our ethical behavior is to be modeled after the life of Christ. See also *hermeneutics*.

congregational hermeneutics: The practice of interpreting the Bible within a community of Jesus-followers. Such a community encompasses the past as well as the present, involves those formally well-educated as well as those who are not, and elevates the voices of those who have historically been marginalized—for example, non-Westerners, African Americans, and women. See also *hermeneutics*.

deuterocanonical: Refers to the secondary status the Roman Catholic Church gave to the Apocrypha. The prefix *deutero-* means "secondary."

exegesis: The process of drawing out meaning from a text that involves paying attention to words, grammar, images, and the original cultural context of the writing. Derives from the Greek word *exegeomai*, which means "to draw out." May be practiced with any writing, including the Bible, and is related to hermeneutics; sometimes *exegesis* and *hermeneutics* are used interchangeably, but exegesis typically deals more with understanding the details of a writing ("What is the passage actually saying?") while hermeneutics deals with interpretation ("What might the passage mean—especially to current readers?").

Hebrew Bible: A term for the Old Testament favored by many scholars, as it seeks to respect the reality that most Jews have only one testament that is their Bible. It does not acknowledge, however, that sections were written in Aramaic and that there is also a Greek translation of Israel's scriptures called the Septuagint.

hermeneutics: The practice of interpreting and finding the meaning of any communication, especially written work. Derives from the Greek word *hermēneuō*, which means "to translate" or "to interpret" (see Luke 24:27; John 1:42). Hermeneutics is related to exegesis, and the terms are sometimes used interchangeably. Exegesis typically deals more with understanding the details of a writing ("What is the passage actually saying?"), while hermeneutics deals with interpretation ("What might the passage mean—especially to current readers?"). See also *Christocentric hermeneutics* and *congregational hermeneutics*.

inerrancy: The belief that there are no contradictions, no scientific errors, and no historical inconsistencies in the Bible.

infallibility: The belief that the Bible does not lead to spiritual error—does not deceive—while recognizing that fallible humans wrote the Bible in cooperation with the Holy Spirit.

Masoretic Text: A version of the Hebrew Scriptures produced in the Middle Ages by Jewish scholars called Masoretes. To guide readers, the Masoretes added vowels and other markings to an earlier Hebrew text that consisted of only consonants. The Masoretic Text is the basis for English translations of the Old Testament and is often compared to the Septuagint.

Pentateuch: The first five books of the Bible: Genesis, Exodus, Leviticus, Numbers, and Deuteronomy. Also known as the Torah. Derived from Greek *pente* (five) and *teuchos* (tool, or case for holding papyri.)

Septuagint (LXX): A Greek translation of the Hebrew Bible compiled around 200 BC. The abbreviation LXX is because of the legend that seventy-two Jewish scholars, independent of each other, developed identical translations of the Torah over the extraordinarily brief period of seventy-two days (seventy-two was rounded to seventy, or LXX in Roman numerals). The apostles and other early Christians relied on the Septuagint; it is quoted frequently in the New Testament.

Tanak: An acronym for Torah, Nevi'im (Prophets), and Ketuvim (Writings), the main sections of the Hebrew Bible. The arrangement of the individual books in each section differs in places from most translations in English and other modern languages.

Torah: Although typically translated as "Law," Torah more accurately means "teaching" or "instruction." It is a word that occurs frequently in the Hebrew Bible, and it also refers to the first five books of the Bible: Genesis, Exodus, Leviticus, Numbers, Deuteronomy, which is also called the Pentatcuch.

Discussion and Reflection Questions

INTRODUCTION

1. What do you think of violence perpetrated by those claiming to believe the Bible? Is violence justified? Why or why not?
2. How has your experience with the Bible given you a sense of what God is like? Of what humans are like?

CHAPTER 1

1. Is there an overarching story in the Bible? How might you summarize it? As a play with several acts? As a story emphasizing various themes?
2. The God of the Old Testament and Jesus in the New Testament are both shown to be Creator, Savior, and

King. Does that reality affect your view of God in any way?

3. Pharaoh, as portrayed in the book of Exodus, represents the way Satan influences humanity. What does it mean that without Jesus, humans are slaves to sin?

4. What is the new creation that the New Testament points to?

CHAPTER 2

1. Christians have long held that Jesus is both divine and human, and called "the Word" (John 1:1-18). Might the Bible represent something similar—a divine and human collaboration? What are some of the implications of such an idea?

2. Does knowing that the Bible is a library, consisting of different styles of writing compiled over time, affect the way you approach it? How so?

3. What are some possible implications of the fact that the Bible was originally written in ancient languages and directed toward ancient peoples?

4. Do you think there is any benefit to studying the Apocrypha? If so, what might it be?

CHAPTER 3

1. What does it mean that "Jesus is the center of the Bible" when reading the Old Testament?

2. How might a "flat" approach to the Bible—where all words are weighted as equally authoritative—lead to oppressive interpretations?

3. How does a Christocentric interpretation of the Bible affect the way we behave?

4. Read Psalm 137. A flat approach to the Bible might understand the end of Psalm 137 to be advocating revenge. Read Matthew 5:11-12, 44. How might Christocentric hermeneutics help us understand the violence advocated at the end of Psalm 137?

CHAPTER 4

1. How might the Holy Spirit be involved in the study of the Bible?
2. What are some differences between reading the Bible academically and reading it devotionally?
3. Does the idea of Spirit-led hermeneutics seem too subjective to you? In what way?
4. Is it possible for an atheist to interpret the Bible?

CHAPTER 5

1. Given that times have changed dramatically in the two thousand or so years since the Bible was written, what value is there in considering the interpretations of ancient Christians?
2. Scholar Barbara E. Reid asserts that "interpreting the Bible is an act of power." Do you agree with that assertion? How is the interpretation of the Bible related to power?
3. The Bible was written by and to marginalized people. Should that fact inform how we read the Bible today? Why might it be important for marginalized people to see themselves in a positive way within the Bible's story?

CHAPTER 6

1. What are some ways that the Bible might be studied in community?

2. Given the emphasis that sermons receive in most worship services, are there ways to reimagine how corporate Bible study can occur in that context?

3. How might things like genre and historical background be helpful in biblical interpretation?

4. Have you observed any benefits for yourself or anyone else when the word of Christ was allowed to "find a home"?

Shared Convictions

Mennonite World Conference, a global community of Christian churches that facilitates community between Anabaptist-related churches, offers these shared convictions that characterize Anabaptist faith. For more on Anabaptism, go to ThirdWay.com.

By the grace of God, we seek to live and proclaim the good news of reconciliation in Jesus Christ. As part of the one body of Christ at all times and places, we hold the following to be central to our belief and practice:

1. God is known to us as Father, Son and Holy Spirit, the Creator who seeks to restore fallen humanity by calling a people to be faithful in fellowship, worship, service and witness.

2. Jesus is the Son of God. Through his life and teachings, his cross and resurrection, he showed us how to

be faithful disciples, redeemed the world, and offers eternal life.

3. As a church, we are a community of those whom God's Spirit calls to turn from sin, acknowledge Jesus Christ as Lord, receive baptism upon confession of faith, and follow Christ in life.

4. As a faith community, we accept the Bible as our authority for faith and life, interpreting it together under Holy Spirit guidance, in the light of Jesus Christ to discern God's will for our obedience.

5. The Spirit of Jesus empowers us to trust God in all areas of life so we become peacemakers who renounce violence, love our enemies, seek justice, and share our possessions with those in need.

6. We gather regularly to worship, to celebrate the Lord's Supper, and to hear the Word of God in a spirit of mutual accountability.

7. As a world-wide community of faith and life we transcend boundaries of nationality, race, class, gender and language. We seek to live in the world without conforming to the powers of evil, witnessing to God's grace by serving others, caring for creation, and inviting all people to know Jesus Christ as Saviour and Lord.

In these convictions we draw inspiration from Anabaptist forebears of the 16th century, who modelled radical discipleship to Jesus Christ. We seek to walk in his name by the power of the Holy Spirit, as we confidently await Christ's return and the final fulfillment of God's kingdom.

Adopted by Mennonite World Conference General Council, March 15, 2006

Notes

Introduction

1 Peter J. Gomes, *The Good Book: Reading the Bible with Mind and Heart* (New York: Harper Collins, 1996), 7.

Chapter 1

1 Quoted in Walter Klaassen, ed., *Anabaptism in Outline: Selected Primary Sources*, Classics of the Radical Reformation 3 (Scottdale, PA: Herald Press, 1981), 155.

2 Kwame Bediako, "Scripture as Interpreter of Culture and Tradition," in *Africa Bible Commentary*, ed. Tokunboh Adeyemo (Nairobi: Word Alive Publishers; Grand Rapids, MI: Zondervan, 2006), 3.

3 Richard Bauckham, "Reading Scripture as a Coherent Story," in *The Art of Reading Scripture*, ed. Ellen F. Davis and Richard B. Hays (Grand Rapids, MI: Eerdmans, 2003), 39.

4 Willie James Jennings, *The Christian Imagination: Theology and the Origins of Race* (New Haven: Yale University Press, 2010), 248.

5 For more on Genesis 3 and how the fall is not emphasized in the Bible, see Walter Brueggemann, *Genesis*, Interpretation: A Bible Commentary for Teaching and Preaching (Louisville: Westminster John Knox Press, 2010), 41–44; and Lloyd Pietersen, *Reading the Bible after Christendom* (Harrisonburg, VA: Herald Press, 2012), 106–7.

Chapter 2

1 The books in the Apocrypha are Tobit, Judith, Esther (Greek version), Wisdom of Solomon, Sirach (also known as Ecclesiasticus, or the Wisdom of Ben Sira), Baruch, Letter of Jeremiah, Prayer of Azariah and the Song of the Three Jews (from the book of Daniel), Susanna (connected to the Greek book of Daniel), Bel and the Dragon (also connected to Daniel), 1 & 2 Maccabees, 1 Esdras, Prayer of Manasseh, and 2 Esdras.

2 Scholars debate the dates that various books were written. Some scholars think a few New Testament writings were written in the early second century, but dating ancient writings is difficult and speculative.

Chapter 3

1 Stuart Murray, *The Naked Anabaptist: The Bare Essentials of a Radical Faith* (Scottdale, PA: Herald Press, 2010), 55.

2 *The Complete Writings of Menno Simons* (Scottdale, PA: Herald Press), 749.

3 Murray, *The Naked Anabaptist*, 69.

4 See Richard B. Hays, *Reading Backwards: Figural Christology and the Fourfold Gospel Witness* (Waco, TX: Baylor University Press, 2014).

5 See Palmer Becker, *Anabaptist Essentials: Ten Signs of a Unique Christian Faith* (Harrisonburg, VA: Herald Press, 2017), 41–43.

Chapter 4

1 In the New Testament, the word *scripture* typically refers to the Old Testament. But 2 Peter 3:16 includes letters of Paul as scripture. In time, the early church would come to view the writings of the New Testament as divinely inspired along with the Old Testament (see chapter 1).

2 Joel B. Green, *Seized by Truth: Reading the Bible as Scripture* (Nashville: Abingdon Press, 2007), 97.

3 Craig S. Keener, *Spirit Hermeneutics: Reading Scripture in Light of Pentecost* (Grand Rapids, MI: Eerdmans, 2016).

4 Quoted in Stuart Murray, *Biblical Interpretation in the Anabaptist Tradition* (North Kitchener, ON: Pandora Press, 2000), 141. The lack of inclusive language was a failure of the time.

5 Craig S. Keener, *Spirit Hermeneutics: Reading Scripture in Light of Pentecost* (Grand Rapids, MI: Eerdmans, 2016), 12.

6 Donald G. Bloesch, *Holy Scripture: Revelation, Inspiration and Interpretation*, Christian Foundations (Downers Grove, IL: InterVarsity Press, 2006), 11.

7 Lloyd Pietersen, *Reading the Bible after Christendom* (Harrisonburg, VA: Herald Press, 2012), 75.

8 N. T. Wright, "How Can the Bible Be Authoritative?," *Vox Evangelica* 21 (1991); 7–32, available online at http://ntwrightpage.com/2016/07/12/how-can-the-bible-be-authoritative/.

9 Quoted in Guy F. Hershberger, *The Recovery of the Anabaptist Vision: A Sixtieth Anniversary Tribute to Harold S. Bender* (Scottdale, PA: Herald Press, 1957), 168.

Chapter 5

1 Barbara E. Reid, "Editor's Introduction to Wisdom Commentary," in *1–2 Timothy, Titus*, Wisdom Commentary 53, by Annette Bourland Huizenga, ed. Sarah Tanzer (Collegeville, MN: Michael Glazier, 2016), xxxiii.

2 Grace Ji-Sun Kim and Susan M. Shaw, *Intersectional Theology: An Introductory Guide* (Minneapolis: Fortress Press, 2018), 70.

3 Peter J. Gomes, *The Good Book: Reading the Bible with Mind and Heart* (New York: Harper Collins, 1996), 18–19.

4 Cited by Brian E. Daley, SJ, "Is Patristic Exegesis Still Usable?" in *The Art of Reading Scripture*, ed. Ellen F. Davis and Richard B. Hays (Grand Rapids, MI: Eerdmans, 2003), 82.

5 Cited in ibid.

6 A couple of resources to consider on this point include E. Randolph Richards and Brandon J. O'Brien, *Misreading Scripture with Western Eyes: Removing Cultural Blinders to Better Understand the Bible* (Downers Grove, IL: InterVarsity Press, 2012); and Emerson B. Powery and Rodney S. Sadler Jr., *The Genesis of Liberation: Biblical Interpretation in the Antebellum Narratives of the Enslaved* (Louisville: Westminster John Knox Press, 2016).

Chapter 6

1 Walter Klaassen, "Anabaptist Hermeneutics: Presuppositions, Principles, and Practice," in *Essays on Biblical Interpretation: Anabaptist-Mennonite Perspectives*, Text-Reader Series, vol. 1, ed. Willard M. Swartley (Elkhart, IN: Institute of Mennonite Studies, 1984), 6.

2 Michael J. Gorman, *Becoming the Gospel: Paul, Participation, and Mission*, The Gospel and Our Culture Series (Grand Rapids, MI: Eerdmans, 2015), 15–16.

The Author

Dennis R. Edwards is associate professor of New Testament at Northern Seminary and the author of *1 Peter* in the Story of God Bible Commentary series. A sought-after speaker at conferences and universities and a frequent contributor at Missio Alliance, Edwards has served as a church planter in Brooklyn and Washington, D.C., and has worked in urban ministry for three decades. Edwards holds degrees from Cornell University, Trinity Evangelical Divinity School, and Catholic University of America, and is ordained in the Evangelical Covenant Church. He and his wife, Susan Steele Edwards, are the parents of four adult children and grandparents of two grandchildren.

SMALL BOOKS
THE JESUS WAY
of RADICAL FAITH

HERALD PRESS

www.HeraldPress.com. 1-800-245-7894